The Open University

ENVIRONMENTAL
• CONTROL • AND •
PUBLIC • HEALTH •

WASTES

Units 8 – 9
Municipal solid wastes management

PREPARED BY THE COURSE TEAM

T237 Environmental control and public health: Course Team

Professor Andrew Porteous	Course Team Chairman	Caryl Hunter-Brown	Liaison Librarian
Judith Anderson	Course Manager	Dr Tony Jolly	BBC
Dr Keith Attenborough	Technology	Dr Andrew Millington	BBC
Cameron Balbirnie	BBC	Dr Suresh Nesaratnam	Technology
Dr Rod Barratt	Technology	Dr John Newbury	Technology Staff Tutor
Lesley Booth	Course Secretary	Dr Brian Price	Unit writing consultant
Dr Keith Cavanagh	Project Officer	Janice Robertson	Editor
Dr David Cooke	Technology Staff Tutor	Ian Spratley	BBC
Sue Dobson	Graphic Artist	Doreen Tucker	Text Processing Compositor
Pamela Furniss	Technology	Bob Walters	BBC
Morine Gordon	Course Secretary	Dr David Yeoman	Unit writing consultant
Caroline Husher	Graphic Designer		

In addition, the Course Team wishes to thank the following for reviewing this material (1992 designations):

External Assessor	Professor Jacob Lewin, Lewin Fryer & Partners, Consulting Engineers
Statistics and epidemiology:	Elizabeth Overton, Public Health Laboratory Services
Wastes:	Colin Palmer, Principal Assistant County Surveyor, Suffolk County Council; John Birch, Managing Director (designate), Lincwaste
Air:	Dr Jimi Irwin, Warren Spring Laboratory

Contents of the course

This text has been printed on Savannah Natural Art™: at least 60% of the fibre used in the production of this paper is bagasse (fibrous residue of sugarcane, a waste byproduct of sugar processing) and the balance is softwood fibre which has undergone an oxygen bleaching process.

The Open University, Walton Hall, Milton Keynes, MK7 6AA.

First published 1993. Reprinted with corrections 1996.

Edited, designed and typeset by the Open University.

Printed in the United Kingdom by Hobbs the Printers Ltd, Brunel Road, Totton, Hampshire SO40 3WX

This text forms part of an Open University Second Level Course. If you would like a copy of *Studying with the Open University*, please write to the Central Enquiry Service, PO Box 200, The Open University, Walton Hall, Milton Keynes, MK7 6YZ, United Kingdom. If you have not already enrolled on the course and would like to buy this or other Open University material, please write to Open University Educational Enterprises Ltd, 12 Cofferidge Close, Stony Stratford, Milton Keynes, MK11 1BY, United Kingdom.

ISBN 0 7492 6174 9

Edition 1.3

13107C/t237u8-9i1.3

UNITS 8–9
MUNICIPAL SOLID WASTES MANAGEMENT

Contents

INTRODUCTION TO THE WASTES MANAGEMENT UNITS

The wastes management units and the associated supplementary material comprise three components, namely municipal, hazardous and nuclear wastes management. The inclusion of 'wastes management' in the titles reflects the overarching aims of this block that wastes ought not simply to be immediately consigned for disposal as if they were of little consequence, but, instead, where environmentally and economically possible, should be minimised and recycled as well.

The components are not equal in length or study requirements. Overall, they span three units and a supplement, and the study time proportions are approximately:

municipal	5
hazardous	2
radioactive	1

spread over the six-week study period allocated to the wastes management units and the radioactive wastes supplement.

The smaller proportion of time allocated to radioactive wastes is not intended to de-emphasise this subject; it merely reflects the fact that municipal and hazardous wastes are an 'everyday' occurrence and their environmental inputs are much greater in volume and complexity than radioactive wastes, whose origins and disposal routes are known and well documented. Radioactive wastes are also handled by a specialist company and thus the opportunities to be involved (or have a say) in their management are much less than for municipal or hazardous wastes from home or industry. The opportunity is also taken in Units 8–9 on municipal solid wastes to establish criteria for landfill site selection and licensing (with special emphasis on groundwater protection) which are common to hazardous wastes as well. We also have to take on board the substantial implications of Part II of the Environmental Protection Act 1990 and its requirements for the future conduct of waste management operations in the UK. You will meet this further in Section 1.2 of the Units 8–9 and in some depth in the legislation supplement.

In order to understand the foundations and principles of UK waste management, the municipal solid wastes units commence with a brief introduction to and overview of legislation which dictates the waste management practices that follow. Landfill is then discussed in depth, as this currently accounts for the disposal of over 90% of British waste arisings, and will always be in use, and as it effectively establishes a disposal cost base against which all other waste management options are judged. We then move on to energy from waste and recycling and the constraints faced in expanding either or both options. Do bear in mind that disposal is a *must*, and recycling, and any other waste modification practice, is an *option*, whose adoption is primarily established by landfill costs and associated environmental impacts.

This sequence allows the obstacles facing the use of intensive recycling and waste minimisation to be viewed in the context of current British wastes management practices, whose associated disposal costs set severe limitations on the viability of materials reclamation from waste. The emphasis of the block is on what is reasonably practicable, consistent with sound environmental protection, and above all on the safeguarding of public health and amenity which are the principal aims of legislation.

Please note that at the time of preparing this material, waste disposal regulations were in a state of flux. This text illustrates best management principles – reference to the Department of Environment and the waste regulation authorities will always be required for the most up-to-date requirements.

AIMS AND OBJECTIVES

Throughout this text, the terms MSW (municipal solid waste) or domestic waste are used interchangeably. The term 'refuse' is embodied in many references. It is still in common use and will also be found in this text.

The aims of Units 8–9 are:

1   to introduce, in the context of environmental control and public health, the subject of management of post-collection municipal solid waste (MSW), the present and projected disposal processes, legislation and future trends.

2   to delineate those areas of the environment on which MSW disposal impinges and outline the steps taken to minimise any adverse effects.

3   to examine the potential for MSW recycling and the factors which influence the decisions to do so.

After studying this text and any relevant portions of the set book (Porteous, 1992), watching the associated television programmes and analysing your waste survey data, you should be able to:

1   Outline the legislative aspects of municipal solid waste management. [SAQs 1, 3]

2   Describe qualitatively and quantitatively the current composition of municipal solid waste and its likely future composition, and the effects this could have on recycling and incineration or waste-derived fuel production. [SAQs 2–9]

3   Describe how landfill sites may be classified, selected and licensed. [SAQs 10–12]

4   Describe how landfilling of municipal solid waste is performed and the precautions that should be taken to protect water supplies and to prevent public nuisance and leachate formation. [SAQs 10, 11, 15, 16]

5   Describe, in chemical and biological terms, the nature of municipal solid waste and the decay processes it can undergo when deposited in a controlled landfill site. [SAQs 9, 13]

6   Discuss the way in which landfill gas (LFG) is generated in a landfill site and the precautions that need to be taken to prevent dangerous emissions. Also, outline the use of LFG as an energy source and the use of landfill site liners for leachate control and groundwater protection. [SAQ 14]

7   Discuss the possible environmental impacts of waste disposal by landfill. [SAQs 17, 22]

8   Describe the process and design requirements of municipal solid waste incineration and sketch a flow sheet for it, identifying where environmental control measures must be taken to prevent another form of pollution occurring, with special reference to air pollution. [SAQs 17–20]

9   Discuss the economic aspects of incineration with energy recovery and the possible markets available for the energy. [SAQs 21, 23]

10   Describe the production of waste-derived fuels, the outline economics, grades of fuels and their probable markets and any difficulties associated with this reclamation route. [SAQs 22–24, 26]

11   Discuss the possible environmental impacts of energy from waste processes. [SAQs 17, 19, 20, 22]

12   Describe the chemical and biological processes that take place during composting and sketch a flow sheet for these processes. [SAQs 6, 25, 26]

13   Discuss the merits of the recycling of municipal solid waste for materials recovery and the general economic constraints which apply to it. Also, outline the debate on the 'best' route for optimum recycling, whether for materials or energy, or both. [SAQs 27–35]

14   Discuss the problem involved in materials recovery from today's consumer goods and the steps being taken to minimise waste production or produce less harmful wastes for disposal. [SAQs 7–9, 28–31, 33–35]

1 MUNICIPAL SOLID WASTE (MSW) — domestic waste / refuse.

1.1 Introduction

You have already been asked to separate and weigh the contents of your dustbin just before the weekly collection as a Unit 4 exercise in statistics and also in preparation for the wastes management units. How much packaging materials (paper, plastics, glass, metals) and vegetable matter does your household generate weekly? Multiply this by the number of households in Britain (22 million) and you now have some idea of the quantities of domestic waste to be disposed of weekly (remember your results may not be typical of the UK 'average' household). Added to this is the waste from offices, hotels, and other 'trade' establishments, and an amount totalling approximately 30 million tonnes per year is the result. These wastes constitute municipal solid waste (MSW); industrial (e.g. factory) waste is not included.

This text covers the field of MSW management from the generation of the waste to the means of effecting its 'pollution-free' and hygienic disposal. However, it would be wrong just to cover existing practice, whether good, bad or indifferent: the way ahead must be based on information currently available. Thus, MSW is also considered as a resource from which useful energy or materials or both may be recovered, thereby assisting materials and/or energy conservation. These aspects are also taken up later in TV 3 and TV 4 which cover energy from wastes, MSW recycling, recycled paper repulping and associated waste minimisation practices in the pulp and paper industry.

A text of this nature is not a manual for all purposes, but it will set out the issues, give them a critical examination and point out the possibilities for resource conservation.

> Refer to the **waste classifications** entry in the set book (under **wastes**). What classes of waste are listed as 'controlled wastes'?

> 'Household; industrial and commercial waste and any such waste.'   as defined by the UK EPA 1990 Pt II

It should be noted that agricultural, mining and quarrying wastes are currently excluded from the controlled classification, despite being much greater in quantity than the controlled wastes listed above.

In other words, a definition of what exactly is waste (in law) is needed, as the above answer shows. However, legislation will only be touched on briefly (in the next section) so that you may better understand the need for, and foundation of, the major upheaval currently being experienced by the British waste management industry. However, before you trip lightly through the law's requirements, read the set book entry on **waste disposal options** for industrial waste (section (iv) under **wastes**). Then try the following exercises. Note: you are not expected to pick up all the meanings of *all* the terms on your first reading. Just get an overview of the options and a feel as to why legislation is required.

> What waste disposal options listed for industrial wastes in the set book are suitable for MSW? (Recall the composition of household waste that you found in your own waste survey.)

> Landfill and incineration.

> What requirements does the paragraph on landfill set out as characterising an acceptable landfill site?

> Strict control, sealed site, checks on the water balance, leachate (polluted water from the waste) treatment, landfill gas controls, sound aftercare programme (which embraces landscaping and monitoring for pollutants after use).

You should now have an inkling of why the scope for abuse is considerable in the landfill of wastes and why the government has introduced the Environmental Protection Act 1990. Now read the *landfill site* entry in the set book.

> On first reading, what strikes you about this entry?

Again, landfill gas and leachate controls are emphasised. Not only that, a possible method of operating a landfill site is listed under items 1–11 in the entry. From this you may conclude that both landfill and any other waste disposal or treatment operations have the capacity for substantial environmental impacts.

Now refer to Figure 1. This shows the effects of a landfill gas explosion at Loscoe in Derbyshire on 24 March 1986. This occurred after landfill gas (which is high in potentially explosive methane) entered the house and was ignited by a central heating boiler. The landfill gas came from a closed landfill site (i.e. all operations had ceased) which contained MSW plus some liquid industrial wastes. The site was legally closed under the then current legislation (Control of Pollution Act 1974). This incident exposed a major loophole in the legislation. Also, further requirements on the need for the protection of water supplies, transportation of wastes and environmental protection in general had become necessary. Thus, more legislation was brought in under the aegis of the Environmental Protection Act 1990 (Part II).

The House of Commons Environment Committee had strong views too, as the brief article from *The Guardian* below shows:

'A Committee of MPs said yesterday they were appalled at inadequate information about Britain's waste tips.

The Commons environment committee said no one appeared to know what was in the dumps or whether they can cope with future demand for waste disposal.

'We have generally been appalled at the poor standard and patchy coverage of the statistics on landfill,' the committee said in a report[a] which examines Britain's ability to implement a draft European Community directive which will harmonise standards throughout the community.

Britain dumps more of its waste (88%) than any other of the European countries studied in the report. It also incinerates the least (11%).[b]

Michael Heseltine, the Environment Secretary, has taken no action against 56 out of the 79 English waste disposal authorities which have failed to draw up waste disposal plans, even though they were legally required to do so 10 years ago.

The committee also urges the Government to guard against the 'wholesale contamination' that is likely to follow because large numbers of smaller landfill operators are expected to shut down and abandon their sites.

Figure 1 *Landfill gas can be dangerous: gas explosion at Loscoe, Derbyshire, 24 March 1986.*

The committee said the Government had no idea whether there is enough landfill capacity and was relying 'upon articles of faith' that the extra 300 000 dry tonnes of sewage, 100 000 tonnes of incinerator ash, and 50 000 tonnes of sludge cake forecast by 1998 can be accommodated.

Sir Hugh Rossi, the Tory MP who chairs the committee, said the proposed EC directive should be welcomed because it aims to raise landfill practices throughout the Community.'

[a]Commons Environment Committee: The EC Draft Directive on the Landfill of Waste; Volume 1, 1991.

[b]2–3% is recycled.

The Guardian, 20 September 1991

1.2 Waste-related legislation – a brief outline

Waste legislation is currently in a state of flux; the Environmental Protection Act (EPA) 1990 has been passed but at the time of writing this material (1992) is yet to be fully implemented. Its stated waste-related aims are 'to make provision for the improved control of pollution arising from certain industrial and other processes; to re-enact the provisions of the Control of Pollution Act (COPA) 1974 relating to waste on land with modifications as respects the function of the regulatory and other authorities concerned in the collection and disposal of waste and to make further provision in relation to such waste...; to amend the Radioactive Substances Act 1960...; to confer powers to obtain information about potentially hazardous substances; to amend the law relating to the control of hazardous substance on, over or under land.'

So, like the 1974 Control of Pollution Act, the EPA is a framework which will be implemented by the introduction of a series of regulations. The full implications of many of the sections of the Act will therefore not be clear until the publication of the necessary regulations.

The Act introduces ***integrated pollution control*** for prescribed industrial, commercial and other processes in England and Wales implemented by Her Majesty's Inspectorate of Pollution (HMIP) and a parallel regime providing for local authority control of air emissions for a second tier of generally smaller scale (and potentially less polluting) processes.

Part I of the Control of Pollution Act 1974 relating to waste on land is replaced by Part II of the Environmental Protection Act with clarified, strengthened and extended controls over waste. Waste disposal licences will be replaced by waste management licences. These are required for the 'treatment, keeping or disposal of controlled waste' – a very embracing statement.

The terms and conditions of the licence relate:

'(a) to the activities which the licence authorises, and

(b) to the precautions to be taken and works to be carried out in connection with or in consequence of those activities.'

Can you think of conditions which might be imposed under (a) and (b) above?

My list includes: e.g., hours of waste facility opening, noise levels, method of storage, transport or treatment, use of qualified staff, distance from housing and protection of ground water by suitable engineering works, leachate and landfill gas control, and an aftercare programme which includes checks on landfill gas and leachate production.

The type of waste that the facilities may treat will also need to be specified. This is not necessarily a simple matter.

Read the ***waste classification*** entry in the set book (section (ii) under ***wastes***, first paragraph and (a) and (b) only).

EPA gives definition of waste

Why do you think the 'simple' definitions given in (a) and (b) in the set book are inadequate?

They do not touch on the origins or the properties of the wastes. For example, clinical wastes need different treatment from household wastes, some industrial wastes may be explosive or carcinogenic, others may react to form toxic gases. This points up the need for more carefully framed definitions and more control of wastes and their handling, treatment and disposal.

Requirements may be imposed in the licence and these are to be complied with *before* the activities which the licence authorises have begun, or *after* the activities which the licence authorises have ceased. Under Section 36, the waste regulation authority (WRA) must also refer the application to the National Rivers Authority (NRA) and the Health and Safety Executive (HSE), and in Scotland the relevant River Purification Authority and the HSE.

Under the EPA, the suitability of a person to be a licence holder will be taken into account when an application is made. The WRA must be satisfied that the applicant is a 'fit and proper person'.

The grounds for refusing a licence under the EPA are widened considerably (compared with those of COPA) to include prevention of pollution of the environment, harm to human health or severe detriment to amenities of the locality.

A licence can no longer be 'handed back' at any time, i.e. surrendered by the licence holder. It may only be surrendered if the WRA accepts the surrender. On an application to surrender a licence, the WRA will inspect the site and may request additional information. 'The Authority shall determine whether it is likely or unlikely that the condition of the land will cause pollution of the environment or harm to human health.' If the Authority is so satisfied, it must then refer the matter to the National Rivers Authority, who may appeal to the Secretary of State if they disagree with the surrender of the licence. Where the surrender of a licence is accepted the Authority will issue the applicant with a Certificate of Completion.

This is a major advance on COPA 1974, where the conditions of the licence cease to be enforceable once the licence is surrendered, regardless of the state in which the land or waste treatment facility is left. This loophole has left several local authorities with massive problems due to past site mismanagement, as, for example, at Loscoe (see Figure 1) where the site licence was legally surrendered and the LFG explosion occurred later.

To what authority must the Waste Regulation Authority refer applications both for a waste management licence and applications for surrender of same?

The National Rivers Authority.

Contravention of the conditions of the waste management licence will be an offence under the Act.

A licence may be revoked by the WRA, if it appears to the authority:

(a) that the holder of the licence has ceased to be a fit and proper person by reason of his/her having been convicted of a relevant offence; or

(b) that the continuation of the activities authorised by the licence would cause pollution of the environment or harm to human health or would be seriously detrimental to the amenities of the locality affected; and

(c) that the pollution, harm or detriment cannot be avoided by modifying the conditions of the licence.

A new issue covered in Part II of the Environmental Protection Act (Section 34) is the establishment of a ***duty of care***[2]. This imposes a duty on any person who imports, produces, carries, keeps, treats or disposes of controlled waste to ensure that the waste is properly dealt with. Breach of the duty will be an offence. The onus is now placed squarely on whoever generates a controlled waste to ensure that it is transported by a registered company to a suitably licensed site.

Those subject to duty of care must take all reasonable measures to achieve certain goals for waste management procedures

The Act provides for the formation of local authority waste disposal authorities to separate the regulatory and disposal responsibilities of the WRA. The issue and enforcement of the waste management licences will be dealt with by the WRAs which will be the County Councils in England and the District Councils in Scotland and Wales. The WRA will have a duty to monitor and secure the safety of closed landfill sites, to keep public registers and to publish annual reports. The collection of household waste is the duty of the waste collection authority (e.g. district councils), which also has a duty to draw up a plan to effect recycling of household and commercial waste in its area.

The EPA is a most comprehensive measure as regards waste on land. Appendix 1 of this text lists the relevant sections of Part II, so that you are aware of the all-embracing scope of the Act. You will also meet Part II again in Unit 10.

European legislation relating to waste also needs to be considered. Some of this is briefly outlined below. Refer to the course legislation supplement for an appropriate update (new EC requirements or modifications to existing ones are currently a recurring feature of the waste scene).

*WRA ⎫
NRA ⎬ now all part of
HMIP ⎭ Environment Agency*

SAQ 1

Why should consultation take place with the NRA before a site licence is issued or handed back? *to protect groundwater as a water resource.*

SAQ 2

Summarise the basic principles of duty of care for controlled waste under the EPA. *See answer*

1.2.1   EC measures

The main EC measure is the 1975 Framework Directive on Waste. This defines waste as 'any substance or object which the holder disposes of or is required to dispose of' by national law. Member states must establish waste disposal authorities which must prepare waste disposal plans and regulate waste disposal undertakings by means of permits, inspections and other forms of supervision. The discharge of dangerous substances into water is controlled by the Framework Directive. The implementation of the Control of Pollution Act brought the UK into compliance with the majority of the articles of this directive.

The Framework Directive is supplemented by other directives which regulate the disposal of particular kinds of waste. The 1976 Directive on the Disposal of Toxic and Dangerous Waste controls the disposal of a variety of wastes listed in an annex to the directive. The 1984 Directive on the Transfrontier Shipment of Hazardous Waste covers the transport by road, water, or air of hazardous waste across national boundaries and requires notification by the waste holder to the competent authority of the state whose territory is to be entered.

The operation of landfill sites is subject to the 1979 Directive on the Protection of Groundwater Against Pollution Caused by Certain Dangerous Substances, which controls discharges into ground water which were not controlled under the Framework Directive. The Groundwater Directive contains a list of substances, similar to the list in the Framework Directive; member states must take steps to prevent or limit the introduction of these substances into ground water.

To drive home why we need waste disposal legislation, try SAQ 3.

The 1991 draft Directive on the Landfilling of Wastes was based on the European and American philosophy of entombment (i.e. sealed sites) of hazardous wastes and was expected to restrict the commonly used UK practice of co-disposal of industrial wastes with domestic wastes to sealed landfill sites (see Unit 10).

SAQ 3

List *your* initial selection of potential forms of pollution resulting from waste disposal by landfill, incineration and recycling operations. (We will meet these topics later.)  *See answer*

2   NATURE OF DOMESTIC WASTE

2.1   Introduction

The composition of domestic waste, as determined by analysis (very similar to the one you have conducted in your household waste survey), is the prime consideration before thought can be given to any process for its disposal or combustion or recycling.

Domestic waste analysis is important because:

1   The nature of the waste influences the mode of collection (note also the mode of collection can influence the amount of waste generated too!).

2   The lives of landfill sites can only be estimated, since changes in composition, density and output per person per week affect site life.

3   The design and operation of waste disposal plant (e.g. incinerators) and waste-derived fuel plants is controlled by the nature of the waste.

4   An assessment can be made of the materials available for recycling or reuse. The prime areas for kerbside collection of recyclables can also be identified.

5   An estimate can be made of heavy metals or other biologically active substances that may affect the future use of reclaimed land on which waste has been deposited or which may need to be legislated for in the future. For example, Sweden now bans long-life batteries in MSW due to their *heavy metals* content. (It has a swingeing deposit on the batteries to ensure their return to point of sale for subsequent safe processing of the toxic materials.) The British Battery Manufacturers Association in 1992 started implementing battery collection schemes to ensure compliance with EC Directive 91/957/EEC which required the separate collection of mercuric oxide, nickel cadmium and lead acid batteries for recycling or separate disposal in appropriate facilities.

2.2   Analysis of domestic waste

Analysis is conducted by passing the waste through screens and classifying it according to a standard format laid down by the Institute of Wastes Management. The sample must weigh more than 1 tonne and/or be collected from not less than 100 premises.

The following classes of housing are usually sampled separately:

(a)   properties with open fires;

(b)   multi-storey flats, all-electric or heated without solid fuel;

(c)   flats and houses in smoke-controlled areas.

The implementation of the Clean Air Act 1956 changed the heating habits of many households; there is now widespread use of central heating, some form of which is estimated to be used by over 80% of UK households. This has brought about major changes in waste composition, largely a reduction in the ash content and an increase in the proportion of paper and vegetable content. However, in those few remaining areas with coal fires, the MSW composition can be dominated by the ash and vegetable matter content.

A detailed breakdown of all the main domestic waste constituents up to 1979 is given in the analyses of household waste figures provided by the Chartered Institute of Public Finance and Accountancy (CIPFA) in Table 1. The end column gives 1989 data collected by the Warren Spring Laboratory. Full information on the conduct of waste analyses is given in the monograph *The Analysis of Domestic Waste* (Higginson, 1982).

Table 1 *National analyses of household waste (weight in kg and % per household per week)*

Classification		1935	1967	1970	1979	1989
Screenings (<2 cm) or dust and cinders	%	56.9	31.0	14.9	12	6.8
	kg	9.7	4.0	2.0	1.37	
Vegetable and putrescible	%	13.7	15.5	24.5	24	28
	kg	2.3	2.0	3.3	2.59	
Paper and board	%	14.3	29.4	36.8	29	30.6
	kg	2.5	3.8	5.0	3.21	
Metals	%	4.0	8.0	9.2	8	7.6
	kg	0.7	1.0	1.3	0.88	
Textiles and manufactured fibres	%	1.9	2.1	2.6	4	1.9
	kg	0.3	0.3	0.3	0.47	
Glass	%	3.4	8.1	9.0	10	9.5
	kg	0.5	1.1	1.2	1.15	
Plastics	%		1.2	1.4	7	8.4
	kg		0.2	0.2	0.76	
Unclassified	%	5.8	4.7	1.6	6	7.2
	kg	1.0	0.6	0.2	0.62	
Total weight per household per week	kg	17.0	13.0	13.5	11.05	n.a.
Density	kg m^{-3}	290	160	146	141.0	n.a.

n.a., not available.

Source: 1935–80 data from CIPFA; 1989 data from Warren Spring Laboratory Publications.

However, as Unit 4 has shown, averages (after Unit 4, you might prefer arithmetic mean) on their own are misleading. Table 2 gives a breakdown of the quantities of paper generated per household from various classes of residence in Glasgow in 1982.

Table 2 *Waste paper generated in Glasgow in different types of premises*

Type of premises	Generation per household per week/kg
Houses and bungalows	3.60
Multi-storey flats	1.86
Tenements	2.15

Source: Anderson, C., Dept of Cleansing, Glasgow, as reported in Ph.D thesis by T. Kin Ho, University of Stirling, 1982.

The data in Table 2 could be viewed as somewhat dated. How much confidence can we still have in them?

Examination of Table 1 shows that the <u>percentage of paper and board products in MSW is virtually constant from 1979 to 1989</u>, hence we may infer that the data are not untypical today. (How does your household compare with the values in Table 2?)

What trend do you detect in domestic waste densities (kg m^{-3}) from Table 1?

Due to the increase in packaging materials and the phasing out of coal fires, the density has decreased from 290 kg m^{-3} (1935) to 141.0 kg m^{-3} (1979). This means that the use of compaction vehicles is necessary for waste collection in order that a full payload can be carried. It also means that bigger dustbins may be required too. What's more, waste compaction on landfill sites is more difficult and costly to achieve.

2.2.1   Waste quantities for disposal

A generally accepted figure is that each person in the UK produces 270 kg of household waste per year, to which must be added bulky packaging and garden wastes. A working national total of 18 million tonnes is obtained. In addition, some 12 million tonnes of commercial waste produced by offices, supermarkets, etc., may also be included in the MSW classification. This totals 30 million tonnes per year, and is the figure we will use when considering using waste as fuel. However, there can be major variations in the amounts produced per person per year in household waste as the data in Table 3 show. Bury uses 'wheely bins' (i.e. household waste containers on wheels). Look at the difference in household waste output. The bulky packaging and garden waste is ending up in the bin too!

There is a lot more waste around than just municipal solid waste, as Table 4 shows.

Table 3   *Estimated household waste output, 1987–88*

Authority	Amount of household waste/ (kg per person per year)
London Borough of Bromley	287
London Borough of Ealing	257
London Borough of Havering	274
London Borough of Redbridge	252
London Borough of Sutton	275
Sandwell Metropolitan District Council	256
South Bucks District Council	256
Bury Metropolitan District Council	333

Source: Townend, W. K. (1990) 'The impact of goods packaging on household waste', *Waste Management*, February 1990. Data from the Waste Disposal Statistics published by the Chartered Institute of Public Finance and Accountancy (CIPFA) 1987–88 estimates.

Table 4   *Estimated annual waste arisings in the UK, 1987–88*

Source	%	Million tonnes
Municipal and medical	4	20
Controlled industrial waste	20	100
Dredged spoil (sea disposal)	2.5	12.5
Mineral waste (land disposal)	27	135
Sewage sludge (sea disposal)[a]	6.5	32.5
Agricultural waste (intensive animal rearing units, silage)	17	85
Agricultural wastes (direct deposition, straw)	23	115
Totals	100	500

[a]Sea disposal to be phased out by 1998.

Source: Data from the Waste Disposal Statistics published by the Chartered Institute of Public Finance and Accountancy (CIPFA) 1987–88 estimates. (Because of the widespread privatisation in the waste industry and the need for confidentiality, waste statistics may become more difficult to obtain in the future.)

MSW/medical wastes only 4% of total waste in UK

Agriculture 40%

The origins of waste handled by the waste disposal authorities are given in Table 5. Note that private sector waste disposal contractor statistics of commercial and industrial wastes are *not* included.

Table 5 *Estimated origins of waste handled by the waste disposal authorities, 1987–88*

Examples England and Wales	Collection authorities/%	Commerce and industry/%	Other waste/%	Household amenity/%	Total/ (million tonnes)
Metropolitan areas	62	9	8	21	3.97
Non-metropolitan districts	45	31	7	17	19.18
London authorities	83	4	5	8	2.89
Total for England and Wales	52	25	7	16	28.24

Source: Data from the Waste Disposal Statistics published by the Chartered Institute of Public Finance and Accountancy (CIPFA) 1987–88 estimates.

SAQ 4

From Table 2, estimate the quantity of waste paper in tonnes per week available for separate collection by (say) charities from 1000 households in each residential classification in Glasgow. From your waste survey, how does your household compare?

Handwritten notes:
$1\,kg = 1 \times 10^{-3}\,tonne$
$1000\,kg = 1\,tonne$
Houses/Bungs : $3.60\,kg = 3.60 \times 10^{-3}\,tonne$
$\times 1000$ households
$= 3.6$ tonnes per week

SAQ 5

Calculate the following, using the most recent figures in Table 1 and the **calorific values** of each domestic waste constituent in the table below. (Note: calorific values, CV, are defined as the amount of heat energy obtained by the complete combustion of unit mass of fuel and measured in megajoules per kilogram. All are on a gross basis.)

(a) What is the national average calorific value per kg of domestic waste?

(b) If the CV of industrial coal is 28 MJ kg^{-1}, what percentage of the CV of coal is the average CV of waste?

Handwritten notes:
$\frac{x}{100} \times 28\,MJ\,kg^{-1} = 11.7\,MJ\,kg^{-1}$
$\Rightarrow x = \frac{11.7}{28} \times 100 = 41.8\%\ (42\%)$

Item	Average calorific value as received[a]/(MJ kg^{-1})	% of total waste	Calorific Value
Dust and cinders	9.6	6.8	$9.6 \times 6.8 = 65.28$
Paper	14.6	30.6	446.76
Vegetable	6.7	28	187.6
Metals	nil[b]	–	
Glass	nil[b]	–	
Rag	16.0	1.9	30.4
Plastics	37	8.4	310.8
Unclassified (wood, shoes, etc.)	17.6	7.2	126.72

Handwritten note: $1167.56 \div 100 = 11.7\,MJ\,kg^{-1}$

[a]Moisture content typically 20–30% by mass.

[b]Taken as zero as they are non-combustible.

SAQ 6

A large waste disposal authority, which has neglected to analyse its waste recently, has to dispose of 500000 tonnes of household waste per year. It could reclaim and sell *all* its waste paper, e.g. for either materials reclamation or fuel. Estimate, using the figures in Table 1, the quantity of paper that can be salvaged from the waste and the resultant savings in waste disposal costs if all waste is landfilled at a 1992 gate fee of £15 per tonne. Comment on the drawbacks of this simplistic approach.

Handwritten notes:
Paper = 30.6% of waste
$\frac{30.6}{100} \times 500\,000$ tonnes $= 153\,000$ tonnes

Waste disposal costs
$500\,000 \times £15 = £7\,500\,000$
paper $153\,000 \times £15 = £2\,295\,000$
$£5\,205\,000$
saving

no collection or transport costs
paper can be marketed?

See answer for discussion
of recycling waste paper

15

2.3   Future trends

The changing nature of domestic waste is clearly illustrated in Figure 2. Changes will obviously continue as lifestyles, packaging and methods of news transmission all change. Several pointers are available:

1 the increasing use of plastic bottles as opposed to glass;

2 the increasing use of prepackaging;

3 electronic news-gathering and transmission;

4 increasing use of electronic storage and access via cheap microprocessors and visual display units;

5 positive incentives to recycle and reclaim materials by separation at source and subsequent uplift at the kerbside or deposition in, e.g. bottle banks;

6 possible further changes in domestic heating (central heating now has over 80% penetration, so further changes in MSW composition may take place very slowly);

7 EC packaging regulations may require or strongly encourage the use of refillable bottles for certain classes of beverages;

8 possible measures for mandatory recycling.

All this means that disposal may not get easier because the waste could be of a much lower density, leading to problems over compaction (see Section 2.2).

Recycling and reclamation may also play an increasing part if this becomes national policy and/or socially or economically worth while.

Waste minimisation in MSW may be difficult to achieve as the options available to the general public are often dictated by manufacturers, the packing industry and supermarkets. This is best illustrated by the demise of the returnable refillable bottle in the UK.

> '90 per cent of all glass containers manufactured are not intended to be refilled. The pattern of supermarket retail trading now established through the United Kingdom does not permit the satisfactory operation of established systems for handling returnable glass containers.'
>
> *(Redfearn National Glass, 1974)*

Having said that individual options for reclamation or recycling MSW materials are restricted, they can nevertheless be implemented. For example, people with gardens large enough can compost their vegetable and garden wastes, but not food or cooked foods because of the possibility of attracting vermin. There are proprietary sealed compost bins on the market which claim to be able to compost all food and vegetable wastes hygienically. Surplus packaging can be declined or handed back to the supplier. (My 'best' example is a perfume which came (a) in a plastic bag, (b) gift wrapped, (c) shrink wrapped, (d) in a fancy cardboard box, (e) in a bottle whose external volume measured 300 ml for 200 ml contents. Oh! it also sat on a 'velvet' lined base!) More use of bottle banks, can banks, plastic bottle banks, where available, all contribute to waste minimisation. On the other hand, the petrol expended in going to the bottle bank could outweigh the energy savings from remelting the bottles – so *special* trips to bottle banks may consume more energy than is saved! There are also severe market restrictions which mean that not all waste paper is recyclable. This is discussed in Section 7.2.

One should not also unnecessarily denigrate the packaging industry. There are clear benefits to be obtained in some instances by materials substitution: for example, plastic can carriers (used for six-packs of soft drink cans), which, when substituted on supermarket shelves for cardboard sleeves, in total weighed 4 kg per 1000 six-packs, and resulted in the elimination of 44 kg of cardboard sleeves per 1000 six-packs. So, the equation 'the use of plastics = more waste' is not by any means true. Plastic bottles are much lighter than glass, but are not normally refillable, hence Germany has a selective deposit on polyethylene terephthalate (PET) bottles to encourage their return to the point of sale so that they may be recycled for materials recovery.

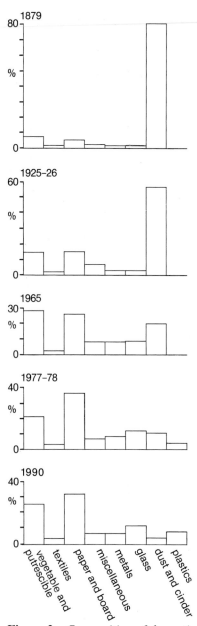

Figure 2   *Composition of domestic waste, 1879–1990.*

Perhaps it is time to bring back the returnable refillable **bottle**. Certainly, it has the potential to save much more energy than the non-returnable glass variety. Table 6 shows the amount of energy required to deliver liquid to the consumer (i.e. not just manufacture the container). We can see that the returnable glass bottle has a good record regarding energy use; so does the PET bottle due to its lighter weight and hence reduced energy requirements for transport.

Table 6   *Systems energy for bottles*

	Returnable glass (10 trips)	Non-deposit glass bottle	PET bottle	Aluminium can	Tinplate can
Container size/ml	550	550	2000	455	455
MJ per container	5	11.2	16.4	6.8	6.1
MJ per litre	9	20.3	8.2	14.9	13.4

Source: Barton, J. (1991) 'Resource conservation v pollution control', *Wastes Management*, September 1991.

What do you conclude from Table 6 regarding the use of aluminium or tinplate cans?

At 14.9 and 13.4 MJ l^{-1} respectively, there is little to choose between them. At 8.2 MJ l^{-1}, the PET bottle is roughly 80% more energy efficient than the aluminium can and 148% more energy efficient than the non-deposit glass bottle (using the 8.2 MJ l^{-1} for PET bottles as the basis of comparison for the efficiency calculations). The returnable glass bottle is the best bet in the energy consumption per litre league if more than 10 trips can be achieved.

Figure 3 shows the trends in packaging in the take-home beer market (the returnable refillable bottle is having a hard time of it in the UK) and Figure 4 shows the trends in the packaging of soft drinks.

Exercise

From Figure 3 and using 1980 as a base, what is the percentage decline in returnable beer bottles by 1986?

Answer

1980 base 15.8% returnables

1986 base 3.3% returnables

Percentage decline = $\frac{(15.8 - 3.3)}{15.8} \times 100$

= 79%

Exercise

What is the percentage growth in PET bottles over this period?

Answer

1980 base PET = 3.5%

1986 base PET = 11.0%

Percentage growth = $\frac{(11.0 - 3.5)}{3.5} \times 100$

= 214%

(handwritten notes in right margin:)

Beer bottles

1980   15.8%

1986   3.3%

$\frac{x}{100} \times \frac{15.8}{100} = \frac{3.3}{100}$

$x = \left(\frac{3.3}{100} \div \frac{15.8}{100}\right) 100$

$= \left(\frac{3.3}{100} \times \frac{100}{15.8}\right) 100$

$= \frac{3.3}{15.8} \times 100$

$= 20.9\%$ ∴ 79.1% decline

PET bottles

1980   3.5%

1986   11.0%

$\frac{11.0 - 3.5}{11.0} \times 100 = 68\%$

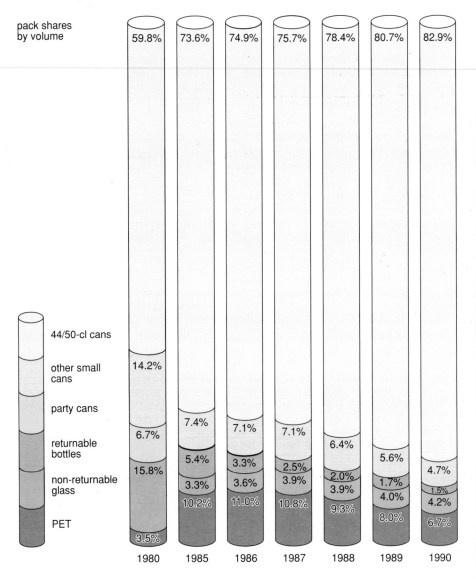

party cans represented 0.1% (1985 and 1986)

Figure 3   *Trends in packaging of take-home beer market.*

SAQ 7

Using Figure 3, how would you characterise the change in packaging for the take-home beer market? Plot the graph number of returnables vs year and extrapolate to 1995.

SAQ 8

Referring to Figure 4 and your graph for SAQ 7, does the percentage reduction in the use of returnable containers for carbonated soft drinks match that of take-home beer over the period 1980–90?

All is not lost, the EC has come to the rescue! More will be said later on in the text on recycling strategies. This is to whet your appetite only!

EC Article 4.1 85/339 on containers of liquids for human consumption is summarised as follows:

Member States shall take measures designed:

(a) to develop consumer education in the advantage of using refillable containers, recycling containers and eliminating used containers from household waste;

(b) to facilitate the refilling and/or recycling of containers of liquids for human consumption;

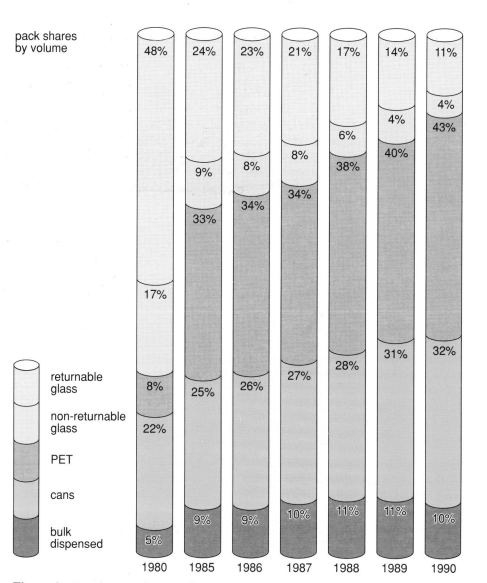

Figure 4 *Trends in packaging of carbonated soft drinks.*

(c) as regards non-refillable containers:

to promote the selective collection of containers,

to develop effective processes for retrieving containers from household waste,

to extend the outlets for materials recovered from containers, in so far as this is economically feasible;

(d) to encourage the technical development and placing on the market of new types of container, with the aim in particular of reducing the consumption of raw materials, facilitating recycling and the final disposal of container waste and achieving overall energy savings;

(e) to maintain and, where possible, increase the proportion of refilled and/or recycling containers and/or to decrease the proportion of non-recycled or non-refillable containers where the conditions of industrial activity and the market so permit.

SAQ 9

Describe briefly the changes that have taken place in the composition of domestic waste over the last 100 years. Suggest reasons for these changes. What are the implications for landfill?

see answer for notes

3   LANDFILL

Now that we know what is in MSW, we need to consider the main method of disposal, i.e. landfill, but to do that we need to know about site licensing, classification and selection. Also, as the UK is a major user of co-disposal for the disposal of many industrial wastes (such as spent acids and sludges) where the wastes are mixed with or discharged into MSW landfills, we need to spend some time on classifying landfills and looking at the impact of their landfill site operations. This will be of use in the later part of the wastes management block which is concerned with hazardous waste management.

3.1   Introduction

Landfill is now the preferred term for the practice that used to be known as controlled tipping. Solid wastes are tipped in layers, compacted, and the layers covered on all surfaces exposed to the air by a minimum specified depth of earth or other suitable material. No waste should be left uncovered for longer than 24 hours. Thus, landfill, properly conducted, should mean an installation where a satisfactory and nuisance-free waste disposal operation is being carried out in accordance with strict control procedures. It is by far the dominant method of household and commercial waste disposal in the UK because of its currently perceived relative cheapness compared with alternatives such as incineration and materials recovery. This is set to change with the advent of the EPA, a perceived shortage of suitable sites (there are plenty of *unsuitable* holes in the ground), and future EC requirements to minimise the environmental impacts of landfill operations.

The avoided cost of *not* landfilling waste can be taken as a recycling credit. (This is the basis of the 'recycling credits' scheme. As an outline example, if the landfilling of waste costs £15 per tonne, a credit of £15 t^{-1} of waste recycled may be payable, or an amount related to the landfill cost which is deemed to be 'avoided' by the collection and removal of recyclable materials from the disposal stream.) Hence, the greater the cost of landfill, the greater the financial incentive to recycle materials from MSW (*given that suitable markets exist*). We can now examine the factors which control landfill operations and why the costs are likely to escalate.

3.2   Site licensing

Section 35 of the EPA (already referred to) requires that a waste management licence be obtained from the Waste Regulation Authority (under the Control of Pollution Act 1974 this is called the Waste Disposal Authority) authorising the treatment, keeping or disposal of any specified description of controlled waste in or on specified land, or the treatment or disposal of any specified description of controlled waste by means of specified mobile plant. The aims of licensing are to prevent:

(a) pollution of the environment;

(b) harm to human health;

(c) serious detriment to the amenities of the locality.

Landfills may be considered as falling into one of three broad types (Waste Management Paper 4 (revised)):

(a) *Multi-disposal*, where a number of wastes are landfilled together but where there is no deliberate aim to make them react together. Some co-reaction (a catch-all term for any chemical activity such as absorption or neutralising that might take place in the mixed wastes) may well take place but this is not prerequisite for the individual waste type to be acceptable for deposit on land. This category includes most household and commercial waste sites as well as a number of industrial waste landfills.

Waste Management Papers are issued from time to time by the Department of the Environment. Appendix 2 of this text gives the 1992 listing.

(b) *Co-disposal*, where limited amounts of certain 'difficult' wastes (solid and liquid) (see **wastes classification** entry) are landfilled with household, commercial and similar wastes from industrial sources.

(c) *Mono-disposal*, where only one type of waste is landfilled, e.g. inert demolition waste (not all demolition waste is inert).

A key part of the licensing procedures is in the working plan which must be appraised before operations can begin. The plan must include attention to the following points:

1   A drawing detailing the engineering development of the site and operational criteria to include:

  specification of boundaries, fencing and landscaping;

  entrance area, gates and signposting, office, weighbridge, wheel cleaning, employee facilities, workshops and maintenance facilities;

  provision of services: electricity, water, sewage and telephone;

  drainage systems;

  internal road system;

  surface water control and drainage system to prevent pollution;

  leachate control and treatment measures;

  monitoring and control systems for landfill gas;

  vermin and insect control;

  odour control;

  dust and litter control;

  materials reclamation procedures;

  accident prevention and safety procedures;

  fire prevention and action procedures.

2   Preparation of work prior to operation:

  hours of opening and operation;

  recording systems for quantities and types of waste;

  staffing levels, including qualifications required;

  progressive restoration system;

  waste processing systems;

  plant and equipment levels and specification;

  discharge methods in windy or wet weather;

  cover material: provision, stockpile, excavation or external supplies;

  any special noise abatement measures required.

3   Restoration plan:

  the land form to be attained on restoration is normally agreed with the Planning Authority at the initial landfill site planning stage; a plan is constructed showing the form and contours of the completed site after anticipated settlement;

  phasing of restoration and contours before settlement;

  progressive drainage systems and final completed system;

  cover and capping details;

  proposed after-use and aftercare, duration

  post-closure monitoring regime (i.e. pollutants to be monitored, frequency of monitoring).

A working plan must take an integrated approach to the numerous aspects of landfill operations because of the complex interrelationships between these aspects.

Engineered landfill requires well-thought-out procedures based on sound technical principles allied with good management.

difficult wastes
- could be harmful to environment
- or physical properties present handling problems.
  eg., acids, alkalis, metals oils, animal/food wastes paint, biocides

3.3   Site classification and selection

Because of the need to protect water supplies, a simplistic nomenclature for hydrological site classification is often used. The three common ones are:

1   Containment sites: those providing a significant element of containment for wastes and **leachates**.

2   Slow attenuation sites: those allowing slow leachate migration and significant **attenuation** (i.e. reduction in concentration or removal of selected hazardous components by dilution and various chemical or physical mechanisms).

3   Insignificant attenuation sites: those allowing rapid leachate migration and insignificant attenuation.

Many sites which provide an element of containment will also permit the slow migration and attenuation of leachates.

3.3.1   Containment sites and leachate seepage calculations

The requirement of these sites is that the leachate be contained. There will always be some seepage which may be calculated as follows (from Waste Management Paper 4, appendix 1 by D.J. Mather):

Consider a clay pit, used as a landfill site, which has an area of 2500 m² (say 50 m by 50 m). The clay is assumed to be homogeneous and, although underlain by sand, does not contain ground water within the sand. No liquids are being discharged and there is a constant head (height) of leachate of 2 m at the base of the waste resulting from infiltrating rainfall. If the clay has a **hydraulic conductivity** or permeability of 10^{-6} m d^{-1}, it is possible to calculate the quantity of leachate seeping (vertically) downwards through the clay using Darcy's law, which can be expressed as

$$Q = kAi$$

$$Q/A = k \times i$$

where Q is the flow rate in cubic metres per day, k is the coefficient of permeability in metres per day, i is the **hydraulic gradient** (defined as head divided by thickness) and A is the cross-sectional area perpendicular to the flow in square metres.

If the clay layer at the base of the landfill is 10 m thick then the hydraulic gradient (i) of leachate across the clay layer is:

$$\frac{\text{leachate height}}{\text{clay thickness}} = \frac{2}{10}$$

and Q is derived as

$$Q = 10^{-6} \times 2/10 \times 2500 \text{ m}^3 \text{ d}^{-1}$$

$$= 5 \times 10^{-4} \text{ m}^3 \text{ d}^{-1}$$

$$= 0.18 \text{ m}^3 \text{ year}^{-1}, \text{ or}$$

$$= 7.3 \times 10^{-5} \text{ m}^3 \text{ year}^{-1} \text{ per square metre of the base of the landfill}$$

By substituting different thicknesses of clay in the above equation, we can get an idea of the influence of this parameter on the flow rate of leachate through the clay and into the underlying sand. Or, if the site is to be lined with an 'impermeable' liner (e.g. butyl rubber which has a very low permeability), and given that the liner permeability and thickness are known, then the leachate flow rate may be calculated. But if the liner has a hole in it, this could make a dramatic difference to the results!

Curve A in Figure 5 shows a plot of flow rate in cubic metres per year, for varying clay thicknesses and a 2-m head of leachate across the base of the landfill whose dimensions are given above. The effect of varying the head of leachate at the base of the landfill is shown in Curves B and C. In Curve B the head has been doubled to 4 m and in Curve C halved to 1 m.

> What flow rate do you predict from Figure 5 for Curve C for (a) clay thickness of 5 m and (b) a clay thickness of 2 m?

> The flow rate is: (a) 0.2 m³ yr⁻¹; (b) 0.4 m³ yr⁻¹.

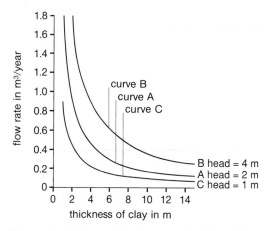

Figure 5 *Relationship between the flow of leachate and the thickness of clay beneath a landfill site with a surface area of 2500 m² for leachate heads of 1 m, 2 m and 4 m.*

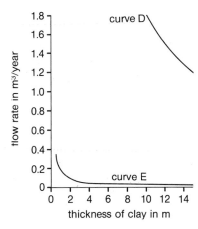

Figure 6 *Relationship between the flow of leachate and the thickness of clay beneath a landfill site with a surface area of 2500 m², for a constant 2-m head of leachate. The permeability of Curve D is 10 times greater than Curve E.*

A similar effect results from variations in permeability. Curves D and E of Figure 6 show the effect of respectively increasing and decreasing the permeability by a factor of 10 for a 2-m head of leachate. From the curves, the benefit to be gained from maintaining a low head of leachate at the base of the landfill and from choosing sites where permeabilities are low or using a low permeability liner is immediately apparent.

There is also likely to be some seepage laterally through the walls of the site. This will be particularly evident if clay is used to cover successive layers of waste as infiltrating rainfall will then tend to move laterally within the landfill.

Containment sites are suitable for solid wastes but not generally recommended for the disposal of large volumes of liquid wastes because of the possible creation of a head of liquid building up in the landfill. Continued discharge of liquids into the site may cause spill-over and hence contaminate surface waters. It is likely that licence conditions will soon limit the maximum head of leachate on a site. If the height is exceeded it must be pumped out and treated. Figure 7 shows a standard leachate-removal chimney for NRA (North West), which must be set at the lowest point of the landfill base, with appropriate drainage connections to it. This shows the engineering measures that are now being enforced in new landfill sites. The 1991 EC draft landfill regulations require that new co-disposal sites be underlain by 3 m of material with a permeability of 10^{-9} m s^{-1} or less in order to effect leachate containment, or that a suitable liner with similar properties be used.

3.3.2 Slow attenuation sites

These sites (e.g. worked-out, dry sand pits with a large ***unsaturated zone*** underneath) allow the leachate to migrate slowly down to the water table and hence be attenuated in its passage through the unsaturated zone. Then trapped air in this zone acts as a ***biological filter*** and enables any organic compounds in the leachate to be broken down.

Slow attenuation sites may be suitable for the disposal of some liquid wastes as these can be degraded, dispersed and diluted before reaching active or potentially active groundwater abstraction zones. An example of such a site given in Waste Management Paper 4 consists of a pit in silt or fine sand, with a permeability of around 10^{-1} (0.1) m d^{-1}, underlain at depth by relatively impermeable clay to protect deeper aquifers (a typical clay permeability is 10^{-6} m d^{-1}).

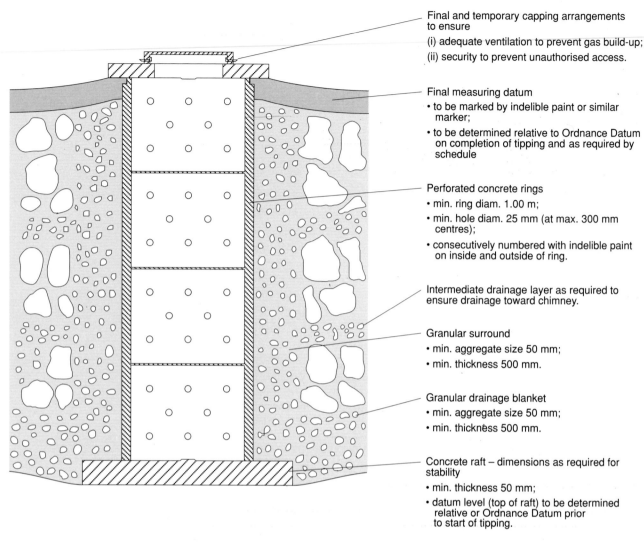

Final and temporary capping arrangements to ensure
(i) adequate ventilation to prevent gas build-up;
(ii) security to prevent unauthorised access.

Final measuring datum
• to be marked by indelible paint or similar marker;
• to be determined relative to Ordnance Datum on completion of tipping and as required by schedule

Perforated concrete rings
• min. ring diam. 1.00 m;
• min. hole diam. 25 mm (at max. 300 mm centres);
• consecutively numbered with indelible paint on inside and outside of ring.

Intermediate drainage layer as required to ensure drainage toward chimney.

Granular surround
• min. aggregate size 50 mm;
• min. thickness 500 mm.

Granular drainage blanket
• min. aggregate size 50 mm;
• min. thickness 500 mm.

Concrete raft – dimensions as required for stability
• min. thickness 50 mm;
• datum level (top of raft) to be determined relative or Ordnance Datum prior to start of tipping.

Figure 7   *Leachate level 'pumping chimney'.*

The groundwater discharge point from the sands would be sufficiently remote to allow ample opportunity for the leachate from the wastes to be degraded and dispersed. Alternatively, ground water within the sands would discharge into a much larger body of water, such as the sea or an estuary, so that any traces of pollutant remaining would be considerably diluted. It should be noted that the NRA view such sites with suspicion and while there are a substantial number currently in use, new applications may not be granted so readily once a groundwater protection policy has been fully implemented.

3.3.3   Insignificant attenuation sites

These sites allow migration of leachates at such a rate that there is insignificant attenuation and hence a greater risk of pollution of ground waters. Such sites may be based on fractured rock or worked out chalk pits with a high permeability.

These sites are only suitable for the disposal of inert materials, in which case monitoring will be required to ensure strict licence compliance so that no illegal or potentially polluting materials (such as toxic timber preservatives) are deposited.

Why should a site receiving only demolition waste be monitored?

(a) Unauthorised hazardous waste disposal can occur.

(b) Demolition waste can contain plasterboard (gypsum) which breaks down to release sulphides which can seriously pollute watercourses.

(c) Timber can also be present which will degrade and form methane over time.

3.4 Site evaluation

Once a potential landfill site has been defined hydrologically, geological and hydrogeological surveys are required to evaluate the site and its suitability to receive various types of waste.

The data required will depend very much on the type and quantity of waste which it is proposed to deposit. It is unnecessary to undertake such surveys at sites where it is proposed to deposit only inert wastes. For sites that are to receive domestic or industrial wastes which, considering their quantity, concentration, etc. are regarded as posing a potential hazard to water supplies, a full hydrogeological survey will be required, which will evaluate among other things:

1   depth of *water table*;

2   water table contour maps for different seasons of the year;

3   magnitude of annual water table fluctuations;

4   location and distance to points of water use.

SAQ 10

A landfill site of area 5000 m^2 is underlain by a layer of clay which is 20 m thick, of permeability 10^{-6} m d^{-1} and is overlain by a head of leachate of 1 m. What is the volumetric flow rate of leachate seeping downwards?

$Q = RAi \qquad k = 10^{-6} \, \text{md}^{-1}$
$\qquad\qquad A = 5000 \, \text{m}^2$
$\qquad\qquad i = \frac{1}{20}$

$Q = 10^{-6} \times 5000 \times \frac{1}{20} = 2.5 \times 10^{-4} \, \text{m}^3 \text{d}^{-1}$

SAQ 11

(a) What do you conclude from Curve C of Figure 5 for a thickness of clay greater than 4–5 m?

(b) What do you conclude from Curves D and E of Figure 6?

3.5 Protection of water resources

As already emphasised, under Section 36 of the EPA, a waste regulation authority is required to refer any proposal to issue a disposal licence to the National Rivers Authority and the Health and Safety Executive. The NRA may request that a licence not be issued, or suggest changes in the conditions to be specified in the licence if it considers that water supplies may be endangered. The potential for conflict between the WRAs and the NRA is evident. Guidelines for the resolution of such issues were devised by the Department of the Environment in a circular entitled *The Balancing of Interests between Water Protection and Waste Disposal* (DoE/Welsh Office, 1976). This was in effect a plea for all factors to be considered in selection of waste disposal sites, plus the acceptance of the inevitability of a small amount of water pollution of a relatively innocuous kind. The implication is that the interested parties, particularly the then water authorities, should consider all aspects before saying that water resources should be protected at all costs, and therefore they should not refuse consent for the landfilling of wastes unless really necessary. This circular was prepared for site licensing under COPA 1974. However, there is evidence that the NRA will now be insisting on highly engineered containment sites as a condition for new waste disposal licenses (see Section 3.5.1). So a much greater degree of protection and monitoring may be anticipated to ensure that the too often cheap and nasty practices of the past are never repeated and water resources threatened. A November 1991 NRA consultation paper (*Policy and Practice for the Protection of Groundwater*) laid out the NRA's initial proposals.

3.5.1 Factors influencing protection of groundwater considerations

Three factors are important when defining the *vulnerability* of groundwater resources to a given pollutant or activity:

- nature of strata;
- nature of overlying soil;
- depth of unsaturated zone.

Vulnerability depends upon the physical circumstances at a location and, in simple terms, provides a measure of the ease with which unacceptable effects upon groundwater resources can take place.

Risk arises when an activity is proposed at a given location. Risk can be mitigated by preventive measures, and different levels of risk will be acceptable depending on the identified vulnerability.

Aquifer
- underground water-bearing layer of porous rock in which water can be stored and through which water can flow.

Any or all of these factors can be relevant in assessing *risk* to groundwater resources. A further factor can be highly relevant:

• proximity to source of pollution,

Nature of strata

The classification of strata may be based on the physical, chemical and biological characteristics of the rock. In practice, these distinctions also reflect the importance of the various strata for water resource purposes.

Aquifers are defined in terms of the rock types which contain ground water in exploitable quantities. (For revision of this term read the entry in the set book and also Unit 7, Section 2.10.) These strata cover about 40% of England and Wales and include a variety of aquifers of different degrees of strategic importance and different hydraulic characteristics (fissured, fissure-porous and porous) and lithology. All ground waters are controlled waters under UK and European legislation and are afforded the same degree of protection. Aquifers may be divided into two types:

1   *Major aquifers* (Type A): These are highly permeable strata, usually with the known or probable presence of significant fracturing. They are highly productive and can yield enough water for large abstractions for public supply and other purposes.

2   *Minor aquifers* (Type B): These can be fractured rocks or potentially fractured rocks which do not have a high primary permeability. Also classed in this category are (a) rocks which are not significantly fractured but are variably porous, and (b) strata where multiple layers of permeable and low permeability rock are interbedded. Although these aquifers will seldom produce large quantities of water for abstractions, they are important both for small local supplies and in supplying base flow for rivers.

Nature of overlying soil

Consideration of the nature of the overlying soil is not relevant where the soil layer has been removed (e.g. landfill, quarrying). However, risk from pollution by activities such as spreading of sludges and manures and from many types of diffuse pollution does depend upon the attenuating characteristics of the soil. We shall not dwell on this important topic, but note that farm activities or sewage sludge spreading on land can give rise to risk as well. Farm wastes were set (1992) to become controlled wastes due to their pollution potential.

Depth of unsaturated zone

The unsaturated zone is that part of the aquifer which lies above the water table. It can play an important role in the attenuation of pollutants, through physical, chemical and biochemical processes, and by acting as a delay mechanism. Travel times through the unsaturated zone can vary depending on the geology and the rainfall recharge. Cracks in the aquifer will allow faster movement whereas rocks where intergranular flow is predominant may slow movement down significantly. The presence of a deep unsaturated zone may be beneficial in protecting groundwater quality, while in fissured limestone strata, for example, little benefit will be gained. For non-degradable pollutants the delay mechanism may only be effective in allowing development of remedial action in the longer term.

Assessing total vulnerability

Figure 8 illustrates two situations where vulnerability varies. The fissured limestone aquifer is an example of high vulnerability whereas the sand and gravel aquifer, overlain by low permeability clay, is much less vulnerable. Not all the above factors are relevant in all circumstances.

Proximity of source of pollution

The proximity of an activity to a groundwater abstraction is one of the most important factors in assessing the vulnerability of an existing groundwater use. All sources, including springs, wells and boreholes, are vulnerable to contamination and need to be protected.

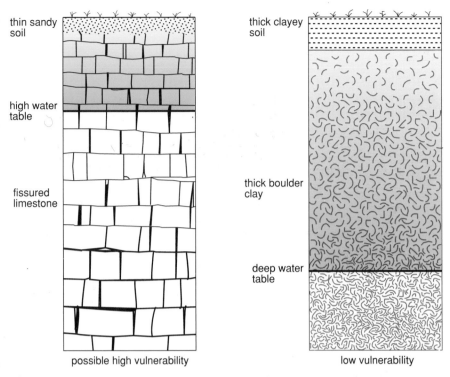

Figure 8 *Examples to illustrate total vulnerability.*

The important factors which could be deemed to pose a threat to aquifers are:

(a) physical disturbance;

(b) waste disposal to land;

(c) contaminated land;

(d) disposal of sludges and slurries to land;

(e) discharges to underground strata.

SAQ 12

Sketch the geological sections of the three main classes of landfill site. Show the possible disposition of the water table and indicate the nature of the strata in each case.

See answer for notes

The degree of engineering now required for MSW landfill sites is shown in Figures 9, 10 and 11, which show the progressive stages in preparing a lined landfill site.

Figure 9 *Prepared cell, prior to liner installation.*

Figure 10   *Liner in situ, but prior to final tensioning.*

Figure 11   *Protection layer being laid on top of liner.*

3.6   *Water pollution control and aquifer protection*

Water percolating through landfill sites leaches out organic and inorganic compounds. This percolated water can leave the site via the subsoil, through culverts or drains or enter static water in which the waste is being tipped. It is undesirable on grounds of amenity (it is offensive) and the fact that it can render any abstracted water unfit for use. Each site is different and consultations with the NRA are required before a land-fill site is commissioned.

This section gives some examples of the methods that have been adopted to contain or prevent water pollution arising from domestic waste disposal sites. The site licence will contain provisions that must be complied with to prevent water pollution. Such requirements are invariably specified by the NRA.

Running water

If a stream runs through the landfill site, diversion or culverting prior to landfill is required as a precaution against water pollution. This is shown in the sequence of

Figure 12 *A site prior to landfill and culverting.*

Figure 13 *Site prior to landfill, culverting completed.*

Figure 14 *Commencement of landfill.*

Figures 12, 13 and 14. The sealing of the pipes is extremely important as any percolation from the site should not be allowed to enter the culvert. If the flow of leachate is very small, instead of costly culverting it may be treated on site (e.g. by aeration) or sent to a sump and pumped to a foul water sewer to a local water pollution control works for fuller treatment. The capacity of the works must be adequate to handle this additional load or any additional treatment plant provided. If this is done on site, the treated effluent may then be discharged to a local watercourse or drain, providing the NRA and the relevant water company agree to this. If the site is near a river bank, culverting or diversion is not possible. In this case, an impervious seal must be inserted between the site and the river bank.

Any run-off from the site must be led to a sump or suitable collection point for treatment or discharge into a foul sewer for subsequent treatment depending on site circumstances. In practice, run-off from a site is often small since water is usually retained in the mass of waste and subsequently evaporates; this is usually adequate to cope with all but prolonged rainfall.

Static water

Precautions must also be taken to prevent static water becoming polluted by tipping. Static water is often encountered in old workings, such as clay pits and quarries. The water should be pumped out prior to landfill, but often this is not or cannot be done. In such cases, the procedure is to infill with inert material (e.g. hardcore) for several metres above the water table to provide an unsaturated base; landfill may then commence.

Underground water

Underground springs, some of which may be undetected at the commencement of landfill, or by prior survey, can force their way through the site and carry highly polluted water with them.

Where this happens, the polluted water should be collected in drains and treated. If springs are known to exist, provision should be made for the spring water to flow through a land drain or pipe wherever possible and the site should be lined with an impervious material, such as clay, or synthetic lining material, prior to landfilling. Polluted water should be conducted from the top of the impervious layer by drains of gravel or ashes and sent to a sewer or removed by tanker for subsequent treatment. The time from the cessation of active landfill to the cessation of treatment of percolated water is an imponderable, but likely to be considerable. A regular monitoring programme will establish the cut-off point.

The sealing of the site from aquifers to ensure the protection of water supplies is most important for sites whose base is above fractured or fissured rocks which would allow the leachate to percolate rapidly to an aquifer. This is well illustrated by the Merstham landfill site in Surrey, where the site was a worked-out lime quarry with a maximum depth of approximately 35 m. The planning permission was granted on condition that the chalk base should be levelled and made impervious, and that soil drainage pipes be laid on the impervious surface and covered with clinker. The open agricultural-type drainage pipes were connected to a cast iron main which led to a storage tank. Hence the leachate is completely drained away and prevented from contaminating the aquifer beneath the chalk.

3.7   Other factors influencing landfill

Site selection considerations are summarised below.

Length of haul (from source of waste to landfill site)

This is usually a major factor in estimating total disposal costs. Conveniently accessible sites have been exhausted for many cities; nevertheless, hauls of up to 50 miles to alternative landfill sites may still prove to be more economical than other means of disposal. (Avon has some of its MSW hauled 100 miles for disposal in Buckinghamshire, but it also has an incinerator.) If long hauls are involved, waste collection trucks may discharge at a transfer station where waste is discharged into specially designed container trucks or trains which haul it to the waste disposal site. It is expected that the use of transfer stations will greatly increase in the future, with the waste being landfilled in large, exhausted, clay pits and other mineral excavation sites which have been extensively engineered. The days of many near-at-hand landfill sites are numbered or have already gone, but their legacy can linger on.

A large increase in the costs of landfill is expected because of:

1 a major increase in standards because of the EPA and pending EC requirements;

2 increased length of haul;

3 the requirements, for aftercare for new landfill sites, incorporated in the Town and Country Planning (Minerals) Act 1981; in addition, the EPA 1990 will require a monitoring regime to be established – this may last 50 years or more for landfill gas monitoring;

4 the need for site monitoring for landfill gas generation for an unspecified period (see Section 3.11);

5 the financing of some form of indemnity or public liability bond for unforeseen consequences after the site is closed.

Public concern has to be taken on board. The article reproduced below from the *Northampton Evening Telegraph*, 1 December 1982, is on Greater Manchester's Council's long-haul waste disposal problems, which is quite typical of the protests made by affected members of the public. This article is reproduced here to give some idea of the amounts of MSW which could have been exported from the Greater Manchester area. (Note the quantity of waste over 15 years.)

Veto on quarry dump scheme

'The plan to dump 1000 tonnes of rubbish a day in quarries near Geddington was kicked out by Kettering planners last night. But the final decision could rest with the Environment Secretary after county planners discuss the scheme next month.

A protest campaign has been mounting since the Evening Telegraph revealed that a similar scheme in Lancashire caused a massive public outcry. Before the committee was a long list of objections, including a petition with several hundred signatures. Councillors heard borough planning officer Mr. Peter Williams spell out what the tip would mean.

About 5.5 million cubic metres of pulverised waste would be dumped over 15 years. New sidings would be built near Storefield Cottages with a rail crossing to Newton Road. A new road would be built across the fields and through the woods behind Geddington. Massive lorries would trek back and forth across the 44 hectare site, transferring huge containers of waste from trains. The operation was two or three times larger than an earlier application agreed in principle. Contrary to previous reports, it would involve wet rather than dry pulverised waste. Leachate – liquid slurry from the waste – could seep from the quarries and pollute the Ise Brook. The proposal was to deal with this by piping it three-quarters of a mile to a sewer near Wood Lane.

Mr Williams told the committee the scheme had no merit whatsoever. It was contrary to the County Structure Plan. It would interfere with agricultural land and the amenities of nearby residents, and there could be traffic hazards because of the nearness of the sidings and Newton Road crossing to the A6003 at Barford Bridge – an accident blackspot. He said the scheme should go to the Environment Secretary as a matter of public interest because it was such a major departure from the structure plan.

Cllr Jim Harker, chairman of Geddington Parish Council, called for an outright refusal on the latest scheme and said no consent should be issued on an earlier smaller application until adequate safeguards were ensured to protect the community.

He said: 'If there is any pollution or smell from that, the operation should cease forthwith.'

The borough should make its strength of feeling known as he understood the county was on the point of giving consent to the earlier scheme. Wrangles with British Steel over plans to use the existing sidings at Glendon had held up that plan and prompted the new more extensive alternative.

Local interest exercise. Go through the back issues of your local newspaper and determine whether your area has protested at planned or existing waste disposal operations.

Mr Williams said the latest information was that difficulties had now been resolved and it was not just a question of reaching financial agreement over the existing sidings.

But councillors condemned both schemes. The mayor, Cllr Terry Freer, said Lancashire should be told to keep its own rubbish. He said: 'We have enough boils on the face of Northamptonshire without a great bleeding ulcer as well.'

Cllr Collete Morgan said it would be a complete disaster for the area and Cllr Ken Gosland said he did not want to see such an activity anywhere in the borough.'

(Northampton Evening Telegraph, 1 December 1982)

(The proposal was eventually dropped.)

Prevention of water pollution

The site should not contain standing water since the combination of decaying waste and water produces extremely offensive smells and encourages the breeding of flies. Running water should also not be present; neither should the site connect with an aquifer, as contamination of groundwater supplies may result (see Sections 3.5 to 3.7). Even if there is no abstraction or catchment for public water supplies near to the landfill, the local amenities should not be destroyed: the decaying organic content of the waste can impose a high *oxygen demand* on any water percolating through the waste or on a connecting stream and render it unfit for fish or other aquatic life.

The crucial role of oxygen in the biological oxidation of organic carbon and nitrogenous materials has been explained in Units 2 and 5–6. The simplified reactions in equations (1) and (2) are included to refresh your memory.

$$\text{organic materials} + O_2 \xrightarrow{\text{microorganisms}} CO_2 + H_2O + \text{energy} \tag{1}$$

$$\text{organic materials} + NH_3 + O_2 \xrightarrow{\text{nitrifying bacteria}} NO_3^- + H_2O + \text{energy} \tag{2}$$

Both these processes utilise dissolved oxygen and, if the dissolved oxygen content of a stream or static body of water is used up, anaerobic conditions can result. In this case, sulphates dissolved from the waste into the water may be used as an oxygen source with consequent reduction to hydrogen sulphide (H_2S) with its characteristically foul-smelling odour and attendant toxic dangers. To prevent this type of action in a properly controlled landfill operation, adjacent streams must be culverted and any static water must be removed.

Distance from housing

The landfill site must be at least 200 m, preferably 500 m, from any housing to avoid nuisance, and assist landfill gas control measures. Noise control and landscaping measures may also be required.

Availability of covering material

In a properly controlled landfill site, the waste is compacted into layers not more than 1.8 m deep and these layers must be covered with at least 180 mm of inert material, such as soil or ashes or thoroughly composted refuse. This prevents or minimises the ingress of flies, rats, gulls and other forms of animal life. The final layer must be covered with 1–1.2 m of subsoil and topsoil to allow cultivation of the land when filling is completed. The covering of the layers of waste is an essential part of the operation, and neglect of this aspect can allow the site to degenerate into a major public nuisance. This has given landfill a very bad name in past years. However, modern compaction methods, if properly used, can do an excellent job. The availability of suitable covering material is now closely examined when planning applications for new landfill sites are made.

Wind

The prevailing wind direction and exposure of the site may make it necessary to erect windbreaks to prevent litter being scattered. Somerset County Council use a completely netted enclosure on their landfilling operations. This concern for litter prevention is to be strongly commended.

In conclusion

Due consideration of the above factors can make landfill an acceptable method of domestic and commercial waste disposal. This method of disposal will continue to predominate for many years, as its costs are currently below those of incineration or other disposal processes. Disposal costs vary with each site, method of working, etc., but typically (1991) lie within the range of £6.00 to £15.00 per tonne of waste for near-at-hand sites.

For long-haul sites, involving the use of, say, transfer stations and specialised truck or rail transport (as practised, for example, by the North London Waste Authority in 1991), the total disposal can cost up to £28 per tonne of waste disposed. When the costs reach this level, other methods such as incineration (Section 4) or waste-derived fuel production (Section 5) may be considered as potentially viable alternatives. The full impact of the EPA and pending EC requirements has still to be felt. Landfill costs can only rise, to which must be added haulage costs.

3.8 The chemistry of domestic waste and its applicability to landfill

The components of domestic waste can be divided principally into 60% organic materials (e.g. food, paper, cloth) and 40% inorganic materials (e.g. ashes, glass, metals). The chemical and biological changes that take place occur almost wholly in the organic constituents (leaving aside such reactions as the rusting of tin cans). When these processes have decomposed a landfill site to an inert mass, it is said to be stable.

> What role do the inorganic materials play in a landfill site?

> They separate the organic contents and can cause uneven distribution. Decomposition may be retarded and stabilisation take longer to achieve.

If, however, all the paper and plastics content were removed, the site could be compacted to a high initial density, but decay processes would still operate on any residual organic wastes, such as food.

The landfill site will not be stabilised until the decomposition of the organic matter by bacterial action has been completed. The complex organic compounds are broken down by the action of bacteria (see Units 1 and 2 on renewal cycles and biological processes) into simpler inorganic chemical forms such as carbonates, nitrates, and carbon dioxide. This process can take 15–50 years or longer, depending on site conditions.

3.8.1 Classes of bacteria

In Unit 2 a method of classifying bacteria was discussed which grouped them according to their oxygen requirements.

1 Aerobes require free molecular oxygen for existence.

2 Obligate (strict) anaerobes cannot exist in free oxygen.

3 Facultative anaerobes are able to adapt themselves to either of the foregoing conditions.

These three types of bacteria are present in landfill sites. The most active in the initial life of the fill are the aerobic type. As time passes, their activity reduces the oxygen content of the air entrapped in the waste. The obligate and facultative anaerobes then take over, although all three types of bacteria may be carrying out their work simultaneously, with varying intensity, in different parts of the landfill.

The result of bacterial action is initial depletion of oxygen and formation of carbon dioxide, leading eventually to anaerobic conditions with consequential associated methane and carbon dioxide production.

Another classification of bacterial activity by Bevan (1967) indicates three well-defined classes of bacteria, each of which is present in a landfill site:

1   *Saprogenic:* These are able to decompose dead organic matter. Bacteria present in ordinary soil, manure heaps and everywhere else where decomposition is taking place may be placed in this group.

2   *Zymogenic:* These bacteria are active in fermentations (i.e. the changes in organic substances induced by microorganisms or enzymes). Bacteria included in this group are often used in commercial manufacturing processes, such as the retting of flax and the preparation of leather.

3   *Pathogenic:* Pathogenic bacteria attack humans and generally cause, or are associated with, human diseases.

3.9   Landfill temperature

The temperature of any landfill increases for a period of time after sealing; 45 °C is quite common and up to 65 °C has been recorded, at which temperature clay landfill caps have been known to crack and destroy the final seal on the site. This is due to the action of aerobic bacteria. The activities of these bacteria reduce the oxygen content of landfill and, eventually, the conditions are such that anaerobic bacteria are able to take over. (This is similar to a compost heap, and, indeed, the composting of MSW as a disposal process is discussed later in the unit, Section 6.)

The temperature rise is normally rapid in the first few days with an increase from the ambient temperatures to a peak in the range 46–71 °C, followed by a gradual decline back to ambient temperature. The total time for this cycle is roughly 15 weeks. The increase in temperature is important to the management of landfill sites in two respects:

1   It shows that decomposition, and thus stabilisation of the organic content, is under way.

2   The temperatures and conditions attained are usually sufficient to eliminate any pathogenic bacteria which may still be present, if they have not already been attacked by the saprogenic bacteria.

The usual practice of tipping the waste (followed by compaction and covering) in 'fingers' or promontories, as shown in Figure 15, assists the aerobic bacteria. The infilling of the bays so created should not be undertaken until the temperature of the fingers has stabilised so that maximum aerobic stabilisation is obtained. The method of landfilling on a slope is shown in Figure 16: you should note the sealing arrangements.

What factors control temperature variation in landfilled domestic waste?

1   Availability of oxygen. This depends on the seal and the distance away from the sides and face.

2   Depth of tipping. Shallow fills dissipate their heat. Heat retention is assisted by deep landfill.

3   Uneven distribution of the organic material.

4   Moisture content also has an effect.

SAQ 13

Give a generalised equation for the aerobic bacterial reactions by which organic matter in refuse is degraded in landfilled domestic waste.

organic matter + oxygen $\xrightarrow{\text{microorganisms}}$ $CO_2 + H_2 + NH_3$ + energy

not? N_2

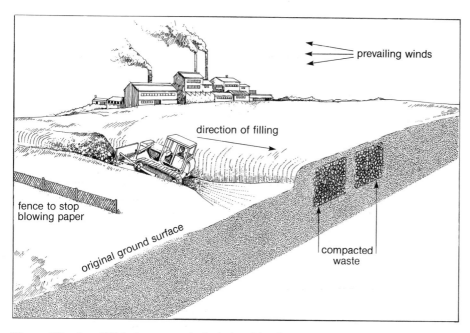

Figure 15 *Landfill in bays on relatively level land.*

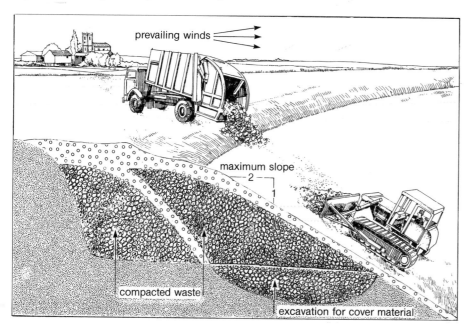

Figure 16 *Landfill in sloping layers.*

3.10 Landfill gas evolution and its control

Gas is released in the anaerobic decomposition processes and, given the changing nature of MSW (i.e. more paper and putrescents, less ash and cinders), it could be a nuisance (or a blessing) depending on whether it migrates to nearby housing or crops or is collected and used as a fuel. Table 7 gives a typical composition of landfill gas (LFG) from one unidentified site near London.

Table 7   *Composition of gas from a former Greater London Council landfill site*

Gas	Composition (%)
hydrogen (H$_2$)	0.01
methane (CH$_4$)	60.83
nitrogen (N$_2$)	2.0
carbon monoxide (CO)	–
carbon dioxide (CO$_2$)	36.09
oxygen (O$_2$)	0.45
hydrogen sulphide (H$_2$S)	trace

Source: Marchant, A.N. (1982) 'The Sweet Smell of Success?' Institute of Wastes Management Spring Meeting, London, 18 March.

Typically, methane concentrations range from 30 to 60%, but 45% is a reasonable working value where continuous extraction is practised as a means of LFG control.

Read the **landfill gas** entry and refer to Figures 54(a) and 54(b) in the set book.

The peak in Figure 54(a) occurs approximately 5–10 years after the end of landfilling operations; thereafter, gas evolves at a decreasing rate. It may be collected by one of several means, all relying on the migration of the gas to a network of ducts similar to that shown in Figure 55(a) and 55(b) in the set book.

If the gas is taken to have an average composition of 45% (by volume) methane, the calorific value is approximately 16 000 kJ m^{-3} (normal) ('normal' means that the gas volume is measured at **normal temperature and pressure** as defined in the set book). Therefore, 2.5 m^3 gas is equivalent to 1 litre of oil as a fuel.

> Why must gas volumes be referred to normal conditions?

> This allows accurate comparisons to be made. For example, if flue gases from combustion exit at 200°C, the gas volume would be 1.73 times greater than if referred to normal conditions, so 1 m^3 of flue gas at 200°C has a lower density than 1 m^3 gas at normal conditions. (Also see Unit 3.)

In Germany, LFG is used for central heating plants for greenhouse and other commercial heating purposes. In the UK, the London Brick Company uses LFG as a fuel in one of its kilns. In this case, the gas is extracted from a large clay excavation pit that has been filled with MSW. This is a good example of integrated waste management as there is a near-at-hand end use for the LFG. Other UK landfill operators generate electricity from LFG. In 1991, there were 18 MW of installed electrical generating capacity powered by LFG. The largest UK household site which receives 10 000 tonnes of MSW per day is installing a 14-MW plant costing £8 million for operation in 1993. The Department of Energy estimates that all the UK's landfill sites could produce LFG equivalent to 3 million tonnes of coal. However, not all LFG can be extracted and used and a substantial portion (up to 70% of LFG generated) still diffuses into the atmosphere, thus contributing to the **greenhouse effect.** Burning LFG does release CO$_2$ which is a greenhouse gas, but a much less powerful one than methane.

There are also many landfill sites where gas collection is not economically feasible and methane migration might be a nuisance (or a downright danger) as in the Loscoe explosion. A variety of methods can be used to control the gas, such as permeable trenches lining the site to allow gases to vent, or a pumped abstraction system using vertical boreholes and interconnecting as shown in Figures 55(a) and 55(b) in the set book, with gas subsequently flared off. As more deep mineral excavation sites are used for landfill, methane migration control or extraction measures will require careful consideration at the planning stage before a licence is awarded.

In serious cases of gas migration, an impermeable gas seal may also be placed around the site to prevent damage to nearby crops or nuisance to the occupants of nearby housing. New sites close to housing could require active LFG extraction (e.g. by vacuum pump) plus rigorous sealing against LFG migration, followed up by monitoring at regular intervals while LFG is being generated.

Landfill gas is also a powerful greenhouse agent because of its methane content. Methane is up to 30 times more powerful (molecule for molecule) than carbon dioxide. UK landfills are estimated to contribute roughly 10% to the UK's total contribution to the greenhouse effect (Department of the Environment Statistics, 1989). We will meet greenhouse gases and their effects later in Units 14–16.

SAQ 14

If a tonne of MSW produces 350 m^3 (normal) of LFG over a span of 30 years in a landfill site:

(a) What is the energy value of this gas assuming an average 45% by volume methane content? $350 \times 16000 = 5600\,MJ$

(b) How does this compare with the energy value of MSW from SAQ 5?

(c) If 30% of the LFG can be extracted for fuel purposes (the rest diffuses to atmosphere), how does this value compare with (b)?

(d) What can be concluded on the use of LFG as a fuel compared with the combustion of 'as received' MSW in an energy-from-waste plant?

The calorific value of LFG (assuming 45% methane content) is 16000 kJ m^{-3} (normal)

The LFG route to energy is not as good as burning MSW for fuel. Due to not all MSW converts to LFG (eg plastic)

— See answer for notes

3.11   Landfill site control and management

Several problems can arise on even the best managed site, including insect and vermin infestations and water pollution.

The common insect pests associated with landfill sites are houseflies, blowflies and crickets. Crickets themselves are not a health hazard, but their noise may be a nuisance.

Flies are a health hazard as they can carry diseases. They are regularly brought to the site in any of their immature forms – eggs, larvae or pupae. Many of these will be buried at sufficient depths to minimise most problems, but if they are deposited near the surface, the larvae may manage to emerge and develop into adult flies. Adult flies may also be attracted to the site if organic matter is left exposed. Good landfill cover is of the essence in insect control.

The standard treatment for these infestations is to spray with **chlorinated hydrocarbon** insecticides. But this practice, when DDT was used, resulted in the emergence of a species of DDT-tolerant flies; thus strict care is required in these control methods.

Rats can also carry disease associated with man, and they may find ideal homes in badly managed landfill sites because poor compaction and voids provide a good medium for burrows. The common means of dealing with rat infestations is poison. Again, resistance has developed in some areas to the 'Warfarin' type of poisons and care must be exercised in rodent control. Good compaction (which with current MSW requires expensive compaction machinery) and good cover again assist in preventing infestation in the first place. If the waste is pretreated by pulverisation or baling, voids can be virtually eliminated and a high standard of hygiene obtained. The use of modern steel-wheel compactor machines can also achieve high densities of wastes on site if properly employed and if the MSW is tipped in thin layers. Where this is not done, loose site densities of roughly 0.7 tonnes m^{-3} occur, compared with >0.85 t m^{-3} where good compaction practices are in use. Some sites claim densities of 1 t m^{-3}, but this may also include cover soil and inert wastes buried in the waste mass. This not only saves landfill space, it assists materially in vermin control. However, some sites are managed for co-disposal purposes (which we will meet in Unit 10) where a larger void space (lower site density) means that more liquids can be absorbed. (There is usually more money in disposing of liquids than in landfilling MSW.)

3.12   Pretreatment by pulverisation or baling prior to landfill

Pulverisation

Pulverisation covers a variety of waste treatment processes which result in the disintegration of the waste from its crude state to a homogeneously sized mix. It is invariably used prior to composting or production of waste-derived fuel, but in this section we shall discuss it from the landfill point of view.

There is a body of opinion which states that crude (i.e. as tipped out of the dustbin) MSW can never be tipped satisfactorily as compaction is difficult with today's low-density, high-volume waste. The proper control of loose material is often difficult, and irregularities in size mean that landfill stabilisation takes longer to achieve unless strict site operational measures are taken and the appropriate compaction machinery is used. Furthermore, cover material in adequate quantities for the sealing of MSW landfills is often just not available and this poses severe landfill management problems.

Pulverisation (as claimed by those few who practise it) gives a homogeneous material with a higher density than compacted waste (1100 kg m^{-3} compared with 850 kg m^{-3}). Compaction is enhanced and less cover material is required.

The pulverisation process itself may be carried out in the wet or dry state. Wet machines are usually horizontally perforated drums which rotate at 12 r.p.m. The size of the perforations, the speed of rotation of the drum, and the time the refuse spends in the drum, control the final particle size. Water is sprayed into the drum to assist the disintegration of the refuse.

Dry pulverisation is usually accomplished by hammer mills. The impact of the hammers effects the reduction of the material. The hammers may be free to swing on one or more rotating shafts, or may be simply fixed to shafts. Hammer mills allow more accurate control of the size of the end product compared with the horizontal wet drum process.

Pulverisation has been used successfully prior to filling in coastal mudflats at Poole in order to reclaim land for road construction. There is no doubt that pulverisation can assist the management of landfill operations, but, again, the question of cost arises as pulverisation may add £6–£8 per tonne to the cost of disposal. Nevertheless, new landfill site compaction machinery and tipping the MSW in thin layers for maximum compaction is eliminating the need for pulverisation in many cases.

Baling

Baling is the compression of the waste into blocks or bales which enables the waste to be easily handled and the landfill site space to be filled without the use of on-site compaction vehicles. Its proponents claim that significant landfill site extension can be achieved due to higher site densities and the need for less cover material. Leachate production may be minimised as well. Also, sites in areas of high rainfall (e.g. Northern Ireland) can be worked all the year round by the use of baling (this may not be possible with loose MSW).

Baling can be either high or medium density, with the end result being a bale weighing around 1.3 tonnes which is easily mechanically handled and stacked in or on the landfill site. Europe's largest two-ram MSW baler was installed at Clayton Hall Quarry, Preston, in 1991 in order to achieve longer site life.

SAQ 15

Given that MSW densities in high-density baling are 1000 kg m^{-3} and that a poorly run landfill site has site densities of 650 kg m^{-3} of poorly compacted waste, by how much longer, and by how many tonnes, will the adoption of baling extend the life of a site with a volume of 200 000 m^3 receiving, on average, 10 000 tonnes of MSW per year?

3.13 The environmental assessment of landfill

[This section is a summary of a paper presented to the Institute of Wastes Management (Marples, 1990).]

Landfill developers have for many years been expected to provide environmental information, in a general sense, when applying for planning permission for a new waste disposal site. This has encompassed hydrogeology, leachate and the prevention of water pollution, and more recently, the potential for LFG migration.

The Environmental Assessment Regulations, introduced in 1988–89 to implement a European Community Directive, place an obligation on planning authorities to consider environmental information before granting permission for certain developments.

Projects described in Schedule 1 of the Regulations (Table 8) always require an *environmental assessment (EA)* to be carried out. These projects include incinerators and treatment works for special waste, and any landfill development involving special waste.

Table 8 *Schedule 1 projects (always require environmental assessment)*

Oil refineries
Power stations
Radioactive waste repository
Steel works
Asbestos works
Chemical works
Roads, railways and airports
Ports and inland waterways
Incinerator or treatment works for special waste (greater than 1 t h^{-1})
Landfill for special waste

Schedule 2 projects (Table 9) only require an EA to be carried out if there are significant environmental effects. These include sites for the disposal of controlled waste or mining and quarry waste.

Table 9 *Schedule 2 projects (require environmental assessment if the development has significant environmental effects)*

Agriculture
Extractive industry
Energy industry
Metal processing
Glass making
Chemical industry
Food industry
Textile, leather and paper industries
Rubber industry
Infrastructure projects
Other projects: holiday village; race track; disposal of controlled waste or mine/quarry waste; waste water treatment; sludge deposition; scrap yard; engine test bed

A DoE/Welsh Office circular suggests that sites to be used for the transfer, treatment or disposal of more than 75 000 t yr^{-1} (tonnes per year or tpy) of household, commercial or industrial waste will fall within the scope of the Regulations.

Schedule 3 of the Regulations sets out the scope of environmental information to be compiled and considered. This includes a description of the proposed development, its likely impact on all aspects of the environment, and the measures to be taken to avoid, reduce or remedy any significant environmental effects.

The developer may also add further explanatory information about the need for the development, the methods used for predicting environmental effects, the adequacy of available information, and so on.

All information must be accompanied by a non-technical summary for the benefit of the lay readership. As well as being read by the planning authorities, the resulting *environmental statement* will become a public document. Both developers and planning authorities should recognise that the process of environmental assessment encourages greater public participation in the determination of permissions for environmentally sensitive projects. (Check with your local planning office and have a look at the environmental statements on file.)

Environmental assessment starts with the identification of key issues. Most of these are already well documented in waste management papers, and include gas migration, leachate migration, landscape, nature conservation, traffic, noise, odour and other nuisances. Site-specific issues, such as the identification of groundwater protection zones, Sites of Special Scientific Interest (SSSIs) and other environmentally sensitive areas, may only become known through discussion with interested parties.

Landfill engineering works should eliminate or reduce to an acceptable level the environmental effects identified at the outset. Each effect therefore needs to be assessed using an accepted expert technique in order to predict the magnitude of the environmental impact. Assessment techniques vary in complexity and sophistication and are listed here for information only. These include groundwater modelling, *event tree analysis* of gas migration, photomontage illustration of landscape changes, and so on. Where appropriate assessment techniques are not available, in areas such as litter and vermin, the developer might evaluate the potential effects by analogy, referring to past performance on existing landfill sites. In each case the developer should be able to demonstrate that the proposed landfill design has evolved in response to a measured evaluation of predicted environmental impacts.

The engineering design and working plan describe how the landfill will be built, operated, restored and cared for after closure. These aspects of the development determine the effect on the environment, and are generally referred to as mitigation measures. These measures need to deal competently with each of the significant effects identified at the outset and, bearing in mind the need for a non-technical summary, should be described using everyday language and illustrations.

The assessment should take account of both direct and indirect environmental effects. The developer should be able to demonstrate that each potential impact is dealt with adequately, and not simply transferred to other parts of the environment.

Measures for dealing with landfill leachate and gas may include sophisticated engineering installations, which should be described clearly in terms of environmental performance. It should be recognised that little can be done to completely eliminate some of the environmental effects of landfill, such as landfill gas and leachate production.

The assessment should describe arrangements for monitoring the environment in and around the landfill and the performance of the proposed mitigation measures. Monitoring needs to encompass all the principal targets (leachate, gas, traffic, noise, nature and nuisances) and embrace the entire active life of the landfill.

Finally, the task of assessing an environmental assessment lies with the planning authority. It must be able to judge the credibility of the descriptive information and, in particular, the environmental predictions offered by the developer. It must also evaluate the feasibility of the proposed environmental engineering works and consider the acceptability of the remaining effects of the development on the environment.

In summary, the environment statement must include the information as noted in Table 10.

Event tree analysis: A formal mechanism for analysing the possible means of LFG migration, weighted by the probability of the occurrence so that control mitigation priorities may be determined.

Table 10 *Requirements of an environmental statement*

Specified information	Explanatory information
Description of the development	Land-use issues
Main environmental effects	Residues and emissions
Impact on: human beings; flora; fauna; soil; water; air; climate; landscape; material assets; cultural heritage	Outline of the main alternatives
	Use of natural resources
	Pollutants, nuisance and waste
Measures to avoid, reduce or remedy significant effects	Forecasting methodology
	Data deficiencies
Non-technical summary for public reference	

The main effects of landfill fall into the following categories:

- gas migration (crop damage, explosion risk and enhancement of the greenhouse effect)
- leachate migration
- landscape and visual amenity
- nature conservation
- road traffic
- noise and vibration
- odour and dust
- litter and vermin
- direct and indirect effects

For completeness (and for background information only), the assessment techniques that may be employed are:

- existing conditions
- monitoring data
- gas migration: event tree analysis
- leachate migration: groundwater modelling
- landscape: photomontage
- nature conservation: ecological analysis
- traffic: waste market analysis
- noise/vibration: equipment specification/propagation modelling
- odour/dust: weather records/dispersion modelling
- litter/vermin: analogy

Mitigation measures include:

- preparation, operation, restoration and beyond
- working plan
- nature conservation

Environmental engineering includes:

- landform
- capping
- containment
- leachate management
- gas management
- surface drainage
- traffic management
- visual screening
- noise attenuation

Monitoring may be necessary in/for the following aspects:

base-line measurement

operational monitoring

aftercare monitoring

active life of landfill

Principal targets:

gas control

leachate control

soil air

surface water

ground water

boundary noise

traffic movement

vegetation and wildlife

odour, dust, litter and vermin

The levels of detail that may be required include:

statement of intent

reference to: standards; codes of practice; guidelines; waste management papers

outline description of works

outline design

working plan

detailed engineering design

You are not expected to be familiar with these techniques, but they are introduced to make it clear that UK landfills are now set to be a thoroughly engineered (and strictly controlled and monitored) means of waste disposal in which high confidence of sound environmental practices can be placed.

It is to be hoped the existing large landfills will be upgraded substantially and small ones closed down. We shall see. The days of the badly run 'council tip' are clearly numbered. Costs will rise as a result of these requirements but this is no bad thing: (a) it will drive out the cowboys due to the capital expenditure required; and (b) it will encourage waste minimisation and recycling.

SAQ 16

(A recap SAQ on the importance of lining.)

Figure 17 shows the flow through a clay liner under 1 m head of water vs liner thickness for permeabilities of 10^{-7}, 10^{-8}, 10^{-9} m sec^{-1} respectively.

(a) If maximum containment is desired, what permeability and liner thickness would you choose, and why? 10^{-9} 2m

(b) If the permeability of the clay chosen changes to 10^{-7} m sec^{-1} due to inadequate quality control, what is the percentage increase in the leachate discharge for a 1-m thick clay liner from your answer to (a)?

SAQ 17

Given that you have not yet met incineration as a disposal method but have been introduced to the EA of MSW disposal by landfill, list the four (to you) most important environmental impacts that could arise from incineration. Do the same for landfill. Are there any common elements?

Incineration	Landfill
Air pollution	landfill gas
noise	water pollution
vehicle movements	vehicle movements
visual intrusion	vermin
	noise
	visual intrusion

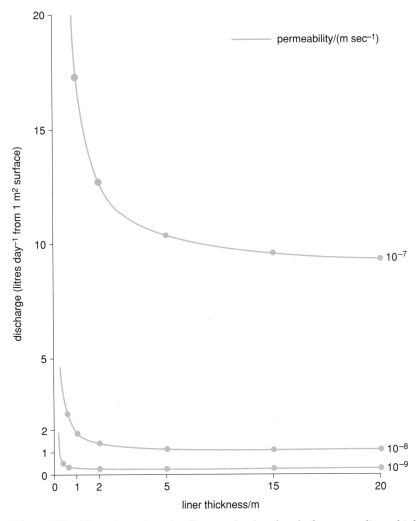

Figure 17 *Flow through a clay liner under 1-m head of water vs liner thickness.*

3.14 Summary of landfill and a preview of incineration

Controlled landfill can be a satisfactory nuisance-free method of disposing of MSW, provided that both high quality site engineering and strict operational controls are exercised. It may also have a useful role to play in the reclamation of derelict land, mainly for recreational or agricultural uses. The composition of today's waste with its high organic content militates against the land being suitable for housing or industry due to LFG production. Aftercare may be a problem as methane generation can continue for 30–60 years after site use is ended. However, with near-at-hand landfill sites becoming harder to find, the trend is towards the use of transfer stations (where large loads of domestic waste are discharged into special containers) or baling so that distant landfill sites can be utilised effectively. This brings with it an attendant increase in costs. New landfill sites will be costly due to the sophisticated engineering works required. Hence, 'energy from waste' using either incineration with energy recovery or the production of waste-derived fuel is also receiving considerable attention as this is a form of recycling (energy recycling) and waste disposal combined. If the costs and environmental impacts associated with these methods compare favourably with those of transfer station plus landfilling, this area of waste utilisation may be expected to grow rapidly.

Television broadcast TV 3 shows how the city of Dusseldorf is tackling its MSW disposal with:

- recovery of materials from MSW for recycling;
- district heating and power generation from MSW incineration;
- recycling of ash and ferrous metal from the incinerator residue;

Recycling of all demolition wastes is also featured.

This means that Dusseldorf is taking a total systems approach to wastes management.

We can now discuss incineration (with energy recovery) as the next method of MSW disposal but one which also conserves energy resources. Thus it may be viewed as a halfway-house between total materials recycling and disposal by landfill. Large land-fill sites can of course extract some of their LFG production economically and use it as a fuel, thus partially utilising part of the energy content of the MSW (SAQ 14 refers).

4 INCINERATION

4.1 Introduction

Incineration (sometimes called mass burning) is the term used for the combustion of municipal and industrial wastes. In a properly designed and operated incinerator there is a substantial reduction in the volume of waste material. The residue (ash) is eventually disposed of by landfill or used for road construction in some countries.

The process is extremely hygienic and many of the problems associated with landfill, such as windblown refuse, rodents and flies, are completely eliminated. Properly incinerated MSW becomes a sterile ash with minimal carbon or fat content and can thus be safely tipped in almost any location provided that dust control measures are taken. (A distinction needs to be made between the grate ash and the fly ash; see set book Figure 52. The grate ash is relatively low in heavy metals whereas the fly ash can be high in cadmium – 370 ppm – and thus is only acceptable at appropriately licensed landfill sites.) The greatest point in favour of incineration is the substantial reduction in bulk: reductions of the order of 90% of the original volume of waste and 70% of its mass are not uncommon.

Incineration can be recuperative, where the heat produced is recovered, or non-recuperative, which currently is the more common in Britain. The term 'energy from waste' is used nowadays for recuperative plants, with incineration reserved for waste destruction only plants. However, there are many energy-from-waste schemes in Europe (one-third of central Paris is heated by using its household waste as a fuel) and several successful installations in the UK: for example, the London Edmonton plant disposes of 380 000 t yr^{-1} of MSW. All new UK schemes are expected to be recuperative, with strict environmental control measures to EC standards.

The basic elements of an energy-from-waste scheme are given in Figure 18. It is seen that there can be up to five waste streams: the incinerator bottom residue, fly ash, quench water, gas scrubber effluent (if a wet process is used) and the flue gases. The principal aspects governing the design of an incineration plant are:

- the nature of the waste;
- the behaviour of the waste in the combustion chamber;
- the nature of the residue;
- the composition of the flue gases.

Now read the **incineration** and **incineration grates** entries and refer to Figure 87 in the set book.

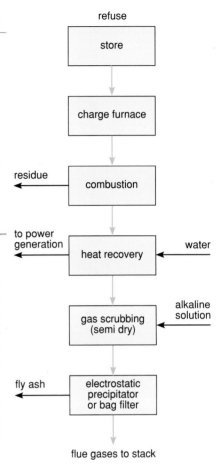

Figure 18 *A flow diagram for recovery of energy from waste using mass burn incineration.*

To test your interpretation of it, how many flue gas scrubbers are in use in Figure 87?

Two. This is a 'wet scrubber' system where the acidic flue gases are 'drenched' by an alkaline solution, which is recirculated for reuse.

What is the purpose of the glass tube heat exchanger?

To warm the cleaned gases before discharge up the chimney. They have been thoroughly cooled in the scrubbers and warming them up increases their buoyancy and eliminates a visual plume of water vapour. You will learn more about this in the air pollution units.

Compare set book Figure 87 with the flow diagram in Figure 18. What are the main differences on the gas cleaning side?

The 'semi-dry' scrubber is applied directly to the exiting gases which are cleaned up in the bag filter afterwards. This will be the usual arrangement for new UK plants. The wet system has dust particles removed (in an electrostatic precipitator) prior to scrubbing.

4.2   The nature of municipal solid waste for incineration

Domestic waste is characterised by its heterogeneity and can range from an old refrigerator to a sackful of bones or a tea-chest of old books. Thus equipment for reducing the size of irregular objects is normally a prerequisite at most incinerator plants. However, as TV 3 makes clear, the design of incinerator grates are such that the burning waste is thoroughly agitated, with sufficient residence time (greater than one hour) in the combustion chamber to ensure complete combustion.

4.3   Combustion of municipal solid waste in incinerators

Combustion of MSW takes place in three stages: evaporation of moisture, distillation and then combustion proper. Evaporation takes place in the furnace due to both radiant and convective heat exchange, and, as further heating takes place, volatile hydrocarbon gases are released with ignition taking place around 700 °C. On further heating (and supplying the requisite amount of oxygen) the *fixed carbon* (i.e. the non-volatilised carbonaceous residue) is consumed and converted to carbon dioxide. The inert, non-combustible matter which remains is discharged to an ash hopper for disposal.

What are convective and radiant heat transfer processes?

Convective heat transfer takes place when heating or cooling is achieved by the circulation of a fluid. In incinerators, convective heat transfer occurs when the hot combustion gases heat the waste on entry to the incinerator. This accomplishes drying prior to combustion.

Radiant heat transfer takes place when heat is exchanged by means of waves (infra-red) between a hot and a cold body. In an incinerator the furnace refractory walls are hot (e.g. 2000 °C), and thus radiant heat exchange plays an important part in the combustion process.

Why is oxygen necessary for combustion?

This is the essence of the combustion processes. Carbonaceous substances, for example, burn according to the reaction given in equation (3).

$$C \quad + \quad O_2 \quad \longrightarrow \quad CO_2 \quad + \quad heat \tag{3}$$

12 g	32 g	44 g	393 kJ

That is, 1 mol of carbon (12 g) requires 1 mol oxygen (32 g) to produce 1 mol carbon dioxide (44 g) and 393 kJ of heat are produced in the reaction (see Unit 3). The oxygen is provided by the combustion air supply. The theoretical air supply is calculated, then an excess (usually 50–80%) allowed to make sure that complete combustion takes place and that little carbon monoxide (discussed further in Units 14–16) is present in the exhaust gases. (This could happen when there is insufficient oxygen to fully oxidise the carbon to carbon dioxide according to equation (3).) Note that coal-fired power stations do not need anything like this amount of excess air. The heterogeneous composition of MSW demands it in order to ensure complete combustion and the absence of 'reducing conditions' (i.e. the presence of *carbon monoxide* (CO) which, in addition to being poisonous, causes thinning of the tube surfaces of the heat recovery boiler.

The air in all combustion furnaces is divided into primary and secondary streams. The primary stream supplies the oxygen necessary for the combustion of the material on the grate. However, volatilisation (in this case, the formation of combustible gases) always take place and the gases and smoke must also be burned: the secondary air stream accomplishes this task. Thus the provision of the correct amounts of air in the primary and secondary streams is of prime importance. Theoretically, the correct amount of air required for combustion can be calculated if the waste analysis is accurate and the composition unvarying. As these quantities cannot be guaranteed and as MSW burns at different rates and can lie on the grate unevenly, up to twice the theoretical amount of air required for complete combustion is supplied to ensure efficient combustion.

What influence will the quantity of volatile matter in MSW have on the distribution of air in a combustion furnace?

The volatile matter is burned mainly by the secondary air stream; thus, the greater the proportion of volatile matter, the smaller should be the ratio of primary to secondary air streams.

The temperature of combustion is important in controlling the odours from dioxin formation in a furnace. Generally, if the gases attain a temperature of 850 °C or above, with a greater than 1 second residence time (2 seconds is specified in HMIP regulations) and appropriate turbulent combustion conditions, *dioxins* are virtually eliminated and odours destroyed.

In any combustion process, *nitrogen oxides* are also formed. We will learn of the problems caused by these in Units 14–16. The aim is to keep them as low as possible through a variety of measures.

The heterogeneous nature of MSW means that it behaves very differently from most other fuels. When paper burns, for example, it forms a protective film that inhibits further combustion; thus a bundle of newspaper will not burn well unless it is agitated. Some materials agglomerate or fuse. MSW combustion requires considerable agitation and a large variety of grates have been designed to accomplish this. If this is of interest to you, a good description of the principal types of incinerator is given by Skitt (1979).

Some grates have rockers which kick up and down; others reciprocate, or use revolving drums, as shown in Figure 53 of the set book under *incineration grates*.

The residue also requires removal. This is usually achieved by discharging it at the end of the grate and then quenching it in a water trough. The quantity and type of ash also influences grit and dust emission, so the design of the gas-cleaning system is crucial.

4.4 Combustion performance and its measurement

Satisfactory combustion should produce a high reduction in volume and also a residue with a low putrescible content. Thus, when the performance of an incinerator is assessed, the putrescible content of the residue and the unburnt carbon is usually tested. Normally, for satisfactory performance, the proportion of unburnt carbon in the residue should be 5% or less. Residual putrescible content is measured by fermentation.

Is there a relationship between the proportions of unburnt carbon and putrescible matter in the residue?

Not necessarily, but a plant producing a residue with, say, 10–15% of unburnt carbon is also likely to produce a residue of high putrescible content which could pollute ground water and/or produce methane when landfilled. Modern installations consistently produce residues with less than 1% unburnt carbon.

SAQ 18

An incinerator residue was found to have an unburnt carbon content of 10%. What are the possible causes?

4.5 Gaseous emission control

The conversion of one form of pollution into another is to be avoided, but with the process of incineration this can easily happen if acid gases and ash particulates are emitted.

Incineration has had a justifiably bad press in the UK in past years. However, all old or obsolete plants are to be shut down by 1996 (in the UK) and all new plant and any old plants after this date have to comply with EC Directive EC/89/369 on their emissions (see *incinerator performance* and Table 9 in the set book). Incineration to EC standards is now a much cleaner (and costlier) operation.

Refer to *incineration performance* and Table 9 of the set book. What combustion conditions does EC/89/369 require for prevention of dioxin discharge? *after Dec 1996? (see Dioxin entry)*

At least 850°C for 2 seconds in the presence of 6% O_2. Note that 'dioxins' are a large family of over 75 chlorinated organic compounds and hence all quoted measurements are made to a TCDD equivalent (see under *dioxins* for explanation. The term 'dioxins' is used ubiquitously, but to be unambiguous, measurements are invariably on a TCDD equivalent basis as itemised at the end of the dioxin entry in the set book.

4.5.1   Dioxins

From Figure 4 in the set book, what is the mean soil concentration (England and Wales) of TCDD?

Approximately 15 ng kg^{-1}.

The control of dioxins from incineration (which are released ubiquitously from garden bonfires, crematoria, house fires, waste oil furnaces and landfill site gas flares) has been tightened up considerably. With appropriate control of combustion temperature and residence time, concentrations can be brought down as low as 0.1 ng m^{-3} in incinerator stack gases, as set out in Table 11. This is one gram in 10 000 000 000 'normal' cubic metres of flue gas, or the metaphorical equivalent of one-quarter of a 3-gram sugar lump dissolved in Loch Ness. (It is a very small quantity!) Note: Refer to the set book to see the concentration at which health effects from *dioxin* were actually experienced in Seveso, to grasp how insignificant 0.1 ng m^{-3} is.

Table 11   *Typical air pollution control standards relevant to the control of 'dioxins'*

Operational parameters	Sweden	Germany	EEC	UK
Temperature (°C minimum)	1200[a]	850	850	850
Residence time (s)		2	2	2
Oxygen content (%)		6	6	6
Emission limits:				
CO (mg m^{-3})		50	100	100
Organics (total C mg m^{-3})	20	10	20	20
Total particulates (mg m^{-3})		10	50	30
Dioxins (ng m^{-3}):				
Existing plant	0.5–2.0			
New plant	0.1	0.1	not stated	1 (guide value 0.1)
Reference conditions[b]	10% CO_2, dry gas	11% O_2, dry gas	11% O_2 or 9% CO_2, dry gas, 273 K, 101.3 kPa	

Note: These conditions may be altered during the lifetime of the course.

[a]For wastes containing polychlorinated aromatic hydrocarbons in levels higher than normal in household waste.

[b]See marginal note for explanation.

Reference conditions. For example, concentrations expressed at 273 K, 101.3 kPa, 11% O_2 or 9% CO_2, dry. This means normal temperature and pressure, 11% by volume O_2 in the combustion gas or 9% CO_2 by volume, to enable comparisons to be made for different plant conditions. 'Dry' means the flue gases have no moisture present when the measurements are made, i.e. the gas sample is dried before the analysis is carried out. We will meet these reference conditions again later in the unit.

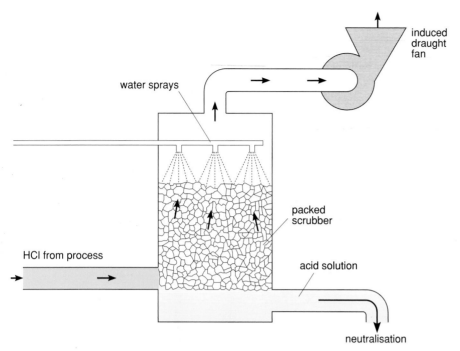

Figure 19 *Diagrammatic wet scrubber for acid fume elimination.*

It is extremely important to control the emissions of the acid gases of hydrogen chloride (HCl), sulphur dioxide (SO_2) – and to some extent hydrogen fluoride (HF) too, although this is a minor component – so it is worth summarising the scrubbing methods available and their respective performance. Figure 19 shows the principle of a basic 'packed bed' scrubber for HCl fume elimination. All scrubbers are variations of this method. In order to prevent blockage from fly ash particles, some form of high-efficiency particulate removal is always employed first if wet scrubbers are used. Semi-dry scrubbers allow evaporation of the alkaline scrubbing medium, which is collected as a component of the fly ash in the particulate removal device afterwards. (We will meet this in Units 14–16.)

What does the packed bed scrubber in Figure 19 do?

Ensures intimate contact of the acid-laden gas with the scrubbing water.

4.5.2   Wet method

Pollutants are removed from the flue gas in an absorption tower (washer) using large quantities of cleaning fluid. Reaction with the absorbents takes place essentially in the liquid phase.

The most frequently applied methods use limestone. Regenerative methods can be used too, with sulphuric acid as the product.

Advantages:

*   high degree of separation (in particular HCl and HF);   *more effective than other two methods for reducing emission of HCl & SO_2*

*   product is generally reusable (e.g. gypsum, sulphuric acid).

Disadvantages:

*   extensive equipment required;

*   flue gas reheating;

*   waste water.

The flue gases from the furnace are conveyed to the flue gas cleaning system by means of induced-draught blowers. Before entering the absorbers, the hot flue gases are usually circulated around regenerative gas preheaters and they transfer some of their heat to the cold flue gases.

Inside the absorbers the flue gases are normally transported against the flow of the cleaning fluid (limestone suspension) and in the process they are cooled down to saturation temperature and cleaned. Following this, the flue gases are reheated in the regenerative gas preheaters before being discharged through the chimney. The necessary limestone powder is mixed in the mixing tank with filtrate from the gypsum drain and pumped to the absorbers.

The reaction in the absorber is represented by:

$$SO_2 + \tfrac{1}{2}O_2 + CaCO_3 \rightarrow CaSO_4 + CO_2$$

Sulphur dioxide + O_2 + limestone → Calcium sulphate + CO_2 (gypsum)

(refer to Unit 3, Section 6 if you need to).

What are the reaction outputs of the wet scrubbing method?

Calcium sulphate $CaSO_4$ and carbon dioxide CO_2.

4.5.3   Dry method

With this method the reaction agent (limestone) is either mixed with the MSW or introduced separately into the furnace.

Advantages:

- little apparatus needed;
- no reheating necessary;
- no waste water.

Disadvantages:

- degree of separation relatively low;
- high limestone demand;
- the reaction product is mixed with ash (disposal problems).

4.5.4   Semi-dry method (spray absorption method)

The absorbent (calcium hydroxide) is mixed with water and sprayed into the flue gas flow. The water evaporates and the pollutants combine with the absorbent to form a dry solid which is removed with the fly ash.

Advantages:

- only slight cooling of the flue gases;
- and possibly no need for reheating;
- higher degree of separation;
- no waste water.

Disadvantages:

- additional apparatus required;
- reaction product not directly reusable;
- (treatment/disposal);
- lime surplus required.

A comparison of the semi-dry vs wet system performance is given in Table 12.

It is likely that the less capital-intensive semi-dry method will be used in the UK as it can readily meet the EC requirements for new incineration plant. This is born out by the before and after results of gas cleaning by the semi-dry method at the Munich North incinerator given in Table 13. (Note: HCl removal can be improved by the use of more scrubbing liquor or longer contact time in the scrubber.)

Table 12 *Comparison of emissions from semi-dry system with those from wet system*

Component	Semi-dry $(mg\ m^{-3})$ (normal) dry @ 11% $O_2{}^a$	Wet $(mg\ m^{-3})$ (normal) dry @ 11% O_2
HCl	50	10
SO_2	100	50
HF	0.5	0.5
Particulate matter	10	10
Heavy metals	1	1
Hg vapour	0.2	0.05

[a]Recall the reference conditions for flue gas measurement in the dioxin section.

Table 13 *Measurements at Munich North incinerator*

Component	Raw gas $(mg\ m^{-3})$ (normal) dry @ 11% O_2	Clean gas $(mg\ m^{-3})$ (normal) dry @ 11% O_2
HCl	600–1500	50
SO_2	200–500	100
HF	5–15	<1
NO	205	160
NO_2	15	10
Particulate	2000–5000	<25
Cd-Ti-Hg	1.3	0.02
As-Co-Ni-Se-Te	4.1	0.15
Sb-Pb-Cr-Cu-Mn	32.5	0.60
Hg vapour	0.08–0.45	0.05–0.2

Basis: gas flow, 120 000 m^3 (normal) hr^{-1} dry; pressure drop, 5 mbar; power requirement per tonne of MSW, 25.0 kWh_e (kilowatt-hour electrical).

Source: McKinley, W. (1989) 'Incineration past and future', Institute of Mechanical Engineering Incineration Seminar, 13 December 1989.

SAQ 19

Refer to the entry on **incineration performance** and Table 9 in the set book for the requirements of EC/89/369 and to Table 13. By how much does the performance of Munich North exceed those of the EC for acid gases and dust discharges?

4.5.5 Flue gas dust

Vogg *et al.* (1986) have examined heavy metal enrichment. Table 14 summarises their work.

Table 14   *Heavy metal enrichment in flue gas dust*

	In refuse/ (g t^{-1})	In flue gas dust/ (µg g^{-1})	Enrichment factor
Ni	100	100	1
Cu	1000	3000	3
Pb	1500	30000	20
Zn	3200	80000	25
Sb	50	3000	60
Cd	20	2000	100
Hg	5	3000[a]	600

[a]The dominant gaseous mercury is considered for better comparison.

Data from Vogg, H. *et al.* (1986) 'The specific role of cadmium and mercury in municipal solid waste incineration', *Waste Management and Research*, 4(1).

These concentrations need to be put in context. Metallic sludges deposited in UK landfill sites, for example, may contain up to 30% zinc. By comparison, Table 14 shows that the percentage of zinc in flue gas dust (the largest component in the ash) is up to 8%, and the cadmium concentration in the ash is 0.2%. UK Waste Management Paper 24 permits the landfilling of cadmium containing wastes from (for example) plating operations where concentrations of up to 2% are to be found. However, incinerator flue gas dust does contain relatively high levels of heavy metals and therefore care must be exercised in its disposal. The heavy metal concentrations in the clinker or bottom ash are generally 1–2 orders of magnitude lower than those of the flue gas dust (fly ash) and hence the fly ash can be mixed with it before being landfilled. However, in the long term, the fly ash may be treated as a special waste requiring disposal in a suitably licensed landfill site. Germany already has pilot plants for the extraction of heavy metals from incinerator fly ash. Other processes immobilise fly ash heavy metals in cement or bituminous matrices. What does emerge from studies is that over 95% of the heavy metals are retained on the fly ash and clinker and are not emitted from the stack. (An exception is mercury which is in the form of a fine aerosol. It should be noted that the principal source of Hg in MSW is from batteries. The British Battery Manufacturers Association plans to have zero mercury content in 99% by weight of British batteries by 1995. This will help eliminate the already small Hg vapour discharges from MSW incinerators.) All EC emission requirements can be readily met in modern well-run plant. All new and existing UK plants will have to meet these requirements. See Table 24 in SAQ 19 answer for the latest HMIP limits (as at late 1992).

SAQ 20

Refer to set book Figure 52.

(a)   What percentage of the total residue does fly ash comprise?

(b)   From Figure 52, if the boiler ash has 0% cadmium and the fly ash 0.2%, what is the composite concentration if both are *thoroughly* mixed before disposal?

4.6   *Economics of landfill vs incineration*

For this course, any economic analysis can only be of a generalised nature to bring out the major factors; therefore, exact comparisons are not possible between (say) landfill and incineration. However, terms of reference for making economic comparisons *can* be agreed. The capital costs of incineration plant are based on 1992 installed costs. Also, landfill prices are not based on historically low levels, but are realistically costed to include both current land acquisition prices and the costs of meeting EPA/NRA measures for new sites. These measures could ensure landfill site gate fees, at 1992 prices, of £12–16 t^{-1}. Haulage and any transfer station costs must be added to these figures.

One estimate of what could constitute realistic landfill prices is given by R. Taylor in a 1989 *Warmer Bulletin* article, reprinted in Appendix 3.

Questions on Appendix 3 'The true cost of landfill – energy recycling is strong competitor'

What MSW site density does the paper postulate?

0.8 tonnes m^{-3}. This increases the December 1988 landfill cost to £9.05 per tonne.

What does the author add to the landfill cost?

Transport of MSW to tip face + wear and tear = £16 t^{-1}.
Future provisions for site sealing and LFG control bring the total cost to £20–21 t^{-1}.

What cost does he postulate for incineration?

£38 t^{-1}.

What has he not costed in the landfill?

Land acquisitions. Note: this now costs up to £5 m^{-3} on new sites. This brings the estimated 1991 landfill cost to about £26 t^{-1}.

This paper is one person's attempt to quantify the costs of landfill. The author has not broken down the costs of incineration, which is seen as a realistic competitor to long haul landfill (1992 landfill costs were up to £29 t^{-1} for hauls of about 60 miles). In addition, there will be substantial LFG control and post-closure costs to be met in the future which the author has not costed. Some offsetting of post-closure costs will be possible for large sites where use can be made of any readily extractable LFG (recall that only 30% can be collected readily).

Table 15 shows a further breakdown of energy-from-wastes costs.

Table 15   *Energy from waste using mass burn incineration costs (1991) for a privately financed 220000 t yr^{-1} installation*

	£ million	Disposal cost (£ per tonne)
Capital cost (including pollution control to better than EC levels)	45	
Operational costs	3.1	
Capital charges (20% return on investment, over 20 years)	9.3	
Total cost (without power generation)	12.4	56.36
Income from electrical power generation at 550 kWh per tonne of MSW based on NFFO tariff of 6.5p per kWh	7.8	
Net cost (with power generation)	4.53	20.59

Comments:

(a)   Up to 600 kWh t^{-1} may be available depending on the calorific value of the MSW.

(b)   Electricity tariff and return on investment are crucial to viability.

(c)   NFFO tariff means non-fossil fuel obligation tariff, which is designed to encourage the construction of electrical power generation plants which do not use fossil fuels. Nuclear power is the principal beneficiary of the NFFO scheme (it received an additional £1.2 billion in 1991 from the NFFO scheme).

Questions on Table 15.

What is the disposal cost without any power generation income?

£56.3 t^{-1}.

What is the disposal cost with 3p kWh^{-1} income?

~~£37 t^{-1}.~~ ? £39 86 t^{-1}

~~What is the disposal cost if the power generation tariff is doubled to 6.5p kWh^{-1} via the NFFO scheme?~~

£21.3 t^{-1}.

From Table 15 it can be seen that the power tariff is a very important factor. As several power generating incinerators (more in the pipeline) and LFG power generating installations are *currently* enjoying non-fossil fuel obligation (NFFO) tariffs of about 6.5p kWh^{-1}, then those waste-to-energy plants (with this largesse) can match current long-haul landfill costs (which are set to rise once the proposed EC landfill regulations are implemented). They can also conserve energy resources and assist in the reduction of the greenhouse effect (the methane in LFG has a greenhouse effect factor of up to 30 times that of carbon dioxide). The NFFO tariff will not last forever and, environmental considerations aside, many decisions will still be made on cost grounds.

However, we can't just go out and install incinerator plants without careful evaluation of their prospects, but it is worth asking why is it that Sweden and Denmark incinerate 65% of their MSW with energy recovery for power and/or district heating while the UK currently incinerates only 3% of its MSW with energy recovery? Television broadcast TV 3 explores this aspect further; but we can say that a new dawn for UK incineration with energy recovery is on the horizon with over 2 million tonnes of MSW capacity planned for the early 1990s in London, Portsmouth and Avon, to name but three. The quoted MSW disposal costs for these proposed plants lie in the range £18–25 t^{-1} as an NFFO power tariff of 6.5p kWh^{-1} is deemed to be available (at least until 1998, but may be extended to encourage the use of non-fossil fuels). Incidentally, wind power has a 1992 NFFO tariff of 11.5p kWh^{-1}. Over 50% of Nuclear Electric's 1991 revenue came from the NFFO levy (it recovered over £1 billion in 1991).

Table 16 gives selected statistics for the Edmonton incinerator in north London.

Table 16   *Selected statistics for Edmonton incinerator in north London, MSW throughput and income figures*

Year	Refuse/tonnes	Total export/MWh	Total income from power sales (£)
1977–78	420 000	187 692	1 520 000
1980–81	399 000	184 053	2 592 000
1986–87	364 560	148 858	4 257 395
1987–88	388 162	157 748	4 164 334
1988–89	344 159	144 744	3 938 320

What can you conclude from Table 16 for Edmonton's income?

It has gone up by 260% (not allowing for inflation) in the period 1977–78 to 1988–89. (It increased further with an NFFO tariff in 1991.)

Edmonton's operating costs have increased over this period, but the bottom line (MSW disposal cost) in 1991 is £12 t^{-1} whereas landfill for north London costs up to £28 t^{-1} due to the use of distant landfill sites. Note that the Edmonton incineration plant has had its capital costs written off and new plants will have higher disposal costs. This is explored later in the text.

We conclude this section on incineration with energy recovery with a comparison of European practices for waste into energy (Table 17). The UK picture is set to change and the associated television programme provides a state-of-the-art update.

Table 17   *European waste into energy comparisons (1991 base)*

Country	MSW incinerated with energy recovery/%
United Kingdom	3
Belgium	7
Denmark	65
France	43
Italy	23
Luxembourg	77
Netherlands	30
Spain	5
West Germany (1990)	35
Sweden	65

SAQ 21

The north London MSW incinerator processed 344 159 tonnes of MSW in 1989 producing 144 744 MWh of electricity for sale.

(a) Calculate the number of tonnes of waste consumed to produce 1 MWh of electricity.

(b) If the waste has a gross calorific value of 10 500 MJ t^{-1}, what is the overall thermal efficiency of the plant where efficiency is ((power output)/(fuel input)) × 100?

(c) How might the efficiency be raised considerably? (Answer this after viewing TV 3.)

(d) Calculate the gross income at 6.5p kWh^{-1} for 1988–89 (from Table 16).

4.7   Summary

Incineration, with energy recovery, in modern well-run plants in a central location with short waste haulage distances is an environmentally sound means of waste disposal, with the added bonus of energy recovery and associated income. Disposal costs can match those of long-haul landfill (whose costs will rise as control measures are tightened under the pending EC landfill directive).

Environmental control measures are such that by 1996 for existing plants (or now for new ones) the stack gas emissions will be better than those from coal- or oil-fired power stations (and much better than car exhausts). This will be discussed in the air pollution units 14–16.

5   WASTE-DERIVED FUEL PRODUCTION

5.1   Introduction

As a half-way house between mass incineration (Section 4) and landfill (Section 3), MSW can be processed to produce a fuel from the combustible waste constituents. The fuel can be either loose (termed a 'floc') or made into pellets (technical name 'densified'.) The major problem is marketability of the product. Also, if you refer back to Table 1, you will see that the readily combustible fraction of MSW totals roughly 40% and something has still to be done with the residual 60% (or more) left after waste-derived fuel (WDF) production.

5.2   Floc fuels

Floc fuels can be fired directly into specially adapted boilers or cement kilns. The pelleted fuels are often used as supplements to solid fuels combustion. (The floc fuel can be used in this way too.)

Now read the **waste derived fuel** entry and refer to Figure 78 in the set book.

> What are the characteristics of the Blue Circle refuse processing flow chart compared with the one in Figure 18 of this text for incineration with energy recovery?

> The flow chart in the set book is much simpler, but is characterised by extensive materials handling as two (power intensive) pulverisers are used plus a vibratory screen. However, the installed capital cost of this installation is considerably less than that of an incinerator with energy recovery as no boiler and power station is required.

Unfortunately, there was only one cement kiln in the UK which used MSW as a fuel. (It has now been shut down for unspecified reasons.) This technology is much more extensively employed in France, which has it on about 8 kilns. It boils down to economics. As the floc fuel has a calorific value of approximately one-half of UK household coal, much more MSW needs to be processed to produce the coal-equivalent replacement floc fuel. The processing costs may go up and coal prices down (as they have done), hence a promising process may be rendered uneconomic. But, it also needs a dedicated installation to burn the floc, so the purchaser of the floc can demand and receive a discount in the fuel price compared with coal.

One way to enhance the economics of floc fuel production is to generate electricity (preferably at the NFFO tariff). This was the basis of an innovative and well-founded planning application in the Merseyside Waste Disposal Authority area; whereby Urban Waste & Power proposed to use **fluidised bed** combustion technology to burn up to 180 000 t yr^{-1} of MSW to generate up to 16.5 MW of electricity for sale to the Merseyside & North Wales Electricity Board at an NFFO tariff. The economics of this process are a commercial matter, but the company has kindly permitted us to reproduce a summary of its Environmental Statement (prepared by L.G. Mouchel & Partners Ltd, December 1990) as set out in Table 18. Note: this is included to illustrate the areas covered in any environmental statement as well as the care needed under EPA. (The applicants were unsuccessful in the 1991 NFFO bidding round.) However, there will be further funding opportunities for renewables in later years.

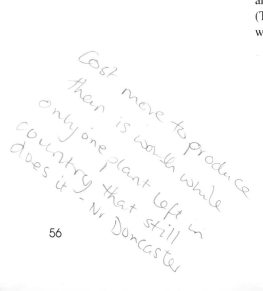
Cost more to produce then is worth while only one plant left in country that still does it - Nr Doncaster

couldn't find market for pellets and pellets had to be landfilled.

Table 18   *Schedule of environmental effects for proposal by Urban Waste & Power for MSW fluidised bed combustion*

Targets	Potential causes of impacts	Mitigating measures taken	Effects upon environment
Humans	Socioeconomic matters	–	Employment prospects increased
	Health risk from pollutants	(see Air below)	–
	Noise	Various attenuation measures.	DOE limits achieved. Little effect
	Odour from refuse	Delivered and handled in enclosed vehicles and building. Negative internal pressure maintained.	None
	Health risk from vermin	Good housekeeping.	None
	Inconvenience due to increase in local traffic	Existing site used and improved junction layout proposed.	Minimal effect
Flora	Pollutants in air	(see Air below)	–
	Land take-up	Existing site used.	Negligible
	Dock water abstraction and discharge at higher temperature	Design for good heat dispersion by dilution and surface cooling. Limitation of discharge temperature.	Minimal
Fauna	Habitat loss due to land take-up	Existing site used.	Negligible
	Pollutants in air	(see Air below)	–
	Noise	Various attenuation measures.	Little effect
	Dock water abstraction and discharge at higher temperature	Design for good heat dispersion by dilution and surface cooling. Limitation of discharge temperature.	Minimal
Soil	Pollutants discharge from stack	(see Air below)	–
Water	Dock water abstraction and discharge	Design for good heat dispersion by dilution and surface cooling. Limitation of discharge temperature.	Minimal
	Changes to land drainage patterns	Existing site used.	Negligible
Air	Dust, fume, acids, heavy metals and organic materials discharged through stack	Clean combustion process uses desulphurisation and dechlorination during combustion.	Latest EC limits achieved
		Flue gas is filtered before discharge. Tall stack for dispersion.	Minimal effect
Climate	Production of carbon dioxide	Combustion process produces less carbon dioxide than fossil-fuel-fired power generation plant.	Negligible
Landscape	Visual intrusion	Existing buildings and chimney used with some addition and improvement.	Beneficial
Interaction between the foregoing	None	–	–
Material assets	Creation of operational plant from currently disused facility	–	Beneficial
Cultural heritage	None	–	–

SAQ 22

Compare the environmental impacts of landfill with those of the proposed Merseyside floc-fired power plant. Are there any similarities? Are there any differences? (Note: plant rejects and ash are sent to a conventional, licensed, landfill site.)

5.3   Pelleted waste-derived fuel production

Floc waste-derived fuel suffers from a very low bulk density and the need for a tied user nearby. Pelleted fuel is a refined form of floc fuel as the floc is further processed then densified or pelleted in a pelleting press.

Read the **pelleted fuel** entry and refer to Figure 68 in the set book. Figure 68 shows the flow sheet for a pelleted fuel plant with an MSW input of 18 tonnes per hour, which produces a 5.2 t h^{-1} output of pellets.

What percentage of the input MSW ends up as pelleted fuel?

About 29%.

This, then, is the 'problem' with waste-derived fuel production. A significant proportion of the MSW is left for disposal or onward processing, e.g. by composting of **fines**, the smallest unused particles (discussed in Section 6). In fact, it is becoming clear that waste-derived fuel production on its own in the UK is a rather risky business if it is not allied with other materials recovery operations such as ferrous metals recovery and composting to improve the economics and reduce the amount of residues sent to landfill. Table 19 gives an economic analysis of a boiler conversion from coal to waste-derived fuel firing.

Clearly, the conversion to WDF firing is a 'good thing' for the WDF user. However, the WDF selling price is assumed to be £20 t^{-1} and, as the flow sheet in set book Figure 68 shows, only 29% of the input MSW ends up as fuel. This means that the gross revenue from pelleted WDF production per input tonne of MSW is only £5.8 t^{-1}, which (plus any waste disposal subsidy) is to pay for the WDF plant capital and running costs, labour costs, electrical power, residue disposal, insurance, rates, etc.

So, WDF production for sale to outside markets is not a high profit business. Where there is an integrated user of the fuel (e.g. the proposed Merseyside plant) then the economics may be transformed as a higher value product (electricity) may be produced. That said, WDF production will have to be allied to other materials recovery practices for it to make much headway.

SAQ 23

Look at Table 19 again.

(a) What is the price per GJ for coal and WDF?

(b) What is the price per GJ output at the boiler stop valve for coal and WDF respectively?

(c) What is the amount of extra ash requiring disposal per year if the boiler is converted to WDF firing?

SAQ 24

(a) From the WDF flow sheet in set book Figure 68, how much of the input MSW requires to be landfilled if all the fines can now be composted and sold together with the ferrous metals?

(b) From the assumed analysis in Figure 68 and the actual output figures on the flow sheet:

   (i)   What marketable 'products' are greater than the analysis and by how much?

   (ii) What marketable 'products' are less than the analysis and by how much?

   (iii) Can you explain the 'discrepancies'?

Table 19   *Economic analysis of boiler conversion to WDF firing*

Boiler size	5.0 MW
Load factor	30%
Capital costs	£50 000
Coal price	£50 t^{-1}
WDF price	£20 t^{-1}
GCV coal	27 GJ t^{-1}
GCV WDF	18 GJ t^{-1}
Coal ash	5%
WDF ash	14%
Coal efficiency	78%
WDF efficiency	76%
Coal ash disposal	£0 t^{-1}
WDF ash disposal	£3 t^{-1}
Extra WDF operating costs	£0.20 GJ^{-1}
Coal costs	£112 308 yr^{-1}
WDF costs	£69 158 yr^{-1}
Fuel savings	£43 150 yr^{-1}
Extra operating costs	£10 913 yr^{-1}
Net savings	£32 237 yr^{-1}
Payback	= 50 000/32 237
	= 1.55 years

GCV, gross calorific value.

Load factor, amount of time boiler is supplying steam over a given period, e.g. 1 year.

Source: Department of Energy workshop on waste-derived fuel in Glasgow on 11 December 1990.

6 COMPOSTING

6.1 The composting processes

Composting is a method of handling and processing 'as received' MSW into a humus-like material which may be used as a soil conditioner or top dressing for a landfill site if carried out with due diligence. However, components such as the fines from WDF production or household vegetables and garden wastes if collected separately are more likely candidates for treatment as they can produce a saleable product for use as a peat substitute; this is just not possible with crude MSW composture due to the presence of glass shards, plastics and heavy metals.

The term composting may also be used (as in the set book) as a name for a biological process of decomposition carried out under controlled conditions of ventilation, temperature and moisture by organisms in the wastes themselves.

Figure 20 shows curves of temperature and pH values plotted against time for a controlled composting cycle. The composting process falls into four readily identifiable stages: mesophilic, thermophilic, cooling and maturing. The decay process commences with the mesophilic stage whose activity decreases as the temperature increases. This eventually ends when the temperature reaches 40 °C. Above 40 °C, during the thermophilic stage, the thermophilic organisms (actinomycetes, other bacteria and fungi) take over, and the pH value of the refuse shows a change to alkaline conditions. Above 60 °C, the thermophilic fungi die, but the actinomycetes can continue to be active. The reaction slows down when the biodegradable materials are consumed. The mass subsequently cools down. Thermophilic fungi then reinvade the waste heap and recommence their attack on the cellulose content, which can take three or four weeks or more to be digested. Eventually, activity decreases and the temperature approaches the ambient. The pH value becomes stable at about 7–8; that is, the material tends to be alkaline. The rate at which the process proceeds is influenced by the size of particles, the availability of nutrients, moisture, temperature and aeration. Typically, a partly matured 'compost' can be made from green wastes (garden waste, fruit, peelings, etc.) in 6–8 weeks. However, 'compost' to the horticulture trade means a growing medium with well-defined characteristics. Many green waste 'composts' are in effect low-value moisture-retaining mulches.

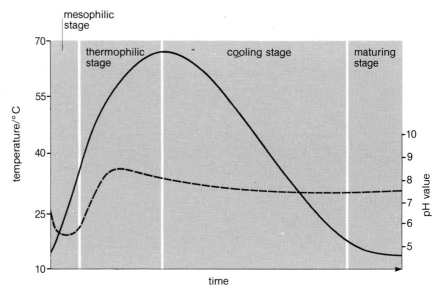

Figure 20 *Graphs of temperature (solid line) and pH value (broken line) vs time for compost manufacture.*

6.2 Composting as a means of domestic waste disposal

Domestic waste composting of mixed (i.e. unseparated waste) is characterised by extensive handling and separation of materials. While many different methods have been developed, there are certain common operations as outlined in Figure 21. Some of the operations shown are optional.

So far, salvaging of materials is not economical (but is done in other European countries), since manual sorting is usually required (an exception is ferrous metals sorted by magnetic means). No strong demand has yet been developed in Britain for the compost and there is great reluctance on the part of municipal authorities to market it, given its high bulk and low selling price. Some schemes have been quoted whereby compost is to be sold as an enriched fertiliser, but farmers have shown little interest in this development. Their reluctance is due, in part, to the fact that basic compost from municipal refuse contains a very high ratio of carbon to nitrogen, or the order of 30:1; this means that its fertiliser content is minimal. This, in turn, is due to the composition of MSW, as nitrogenous compounds are almost non-existent. This problem was overcome at the Wanlip composting plant operated by Leicester County Council by adding sewage sludge to the compost, but there could still be objections to ground glass shards in the product. Unfortunately, Wanlip was closed in 1984 as large quarries adjacent to the City of Leicester became available for low cost landfill, and there was also little demand for the compost.

However, composting is widely practised in EC countries (Holland about 25%) and interest is being shown in separately composting the collected vegetable and putrescible content of MSW and the fines from waste screening arising at waste-derived fuel plants. Hence, both fuel and compost would be available as potentially marketable products, thus substantially reducing the amount sent to disposal by landfill.

What factors militate against the use of compost for agricultural purposes?

The carbon–nitrogen ratio is high (i.e. the fertiliser content is minimal).

Glass, metal or plastic shards can be present and livestock may eat the harmful material or be injured while grazing.

Heavy metals are present in all domestic refuse (e.g. lead, zinc, cadmium) and this could lead to them being taken up by crops or livestock.

After composting, 50–60% of the original volume of the waste remains to be disposed of either by sale or landfill. Compost is not a stable material, and is unsuitable for heavy building or road construction. It can, however, be spread in many localities where crude MSW, even under exacting landfill conditions, is quite unsuitable.

Possible sources of revenue from municipal compost plants are the sales of salvaged material and compost for use as a soil conditioner. However, because of the marketing problems some plants have been replaced by landfill or incineration operations. That said, at the time of writing, large-scale experiments are under way (in suburban areas) to enable households to compost their food and vegetable matter for use in or on their gardens as a means of MSW reduction at source. Some other schemes collect food and vegetable wastes separately and compost them at a control plant. Verifiable costs are not yet to hand.

The composting process is widely used in the Middle East as a means of waste disposal with a highly valued soil conditioner as the end produce. However, the waste analysis varies significantly from the UK in that there is a greater percentage of vegetable matter present. Also, the fines from WDF plants may be eminently suitable for composting. As with all recycling processes (except electricity generation from waste), markets have to be developed for the product(s). This is a major constraint on composting which should not be underestimated. In particular, the horticulture trade is very demanding in its specifications.

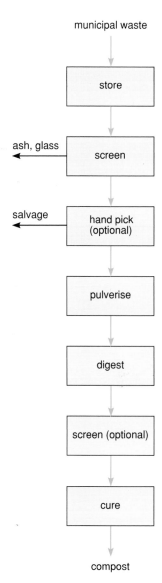

Figure 21 *A flow diagram for the composting of refuse.*

SAQ 25

Figure 20 shows the graph of temperature against time for the process of composting. If the time taken to reach the maturing stage is six weeks, what area of land will be required to store the compost from a plant of 100 tonnes per day capacity (7 days per week operation) in a layer 2 m thick? Assume that the density of the compost is 500 kg m^{-3} and allow a factor of 2 for the space required for materials handling.

SAQ 26

Refer to Table 1. If a waste-derived fuel plant can make fuel from *all* the paper and plastics content, and if *all* the fines and putrescible matter can be composted, what is the percentage by weight left for landfill?

7 MATERIALS RECOVERY

7.1 *Introduction*

We have covered, in the previous sections, landfill, incineration with energy recovery, waste-derived fuels and composting respectively. We now come to what may be perceived as the 'only solution to waste disposal' – materials recovery. Unfortunately, life is not so simple; there are very real restraints as to what may be recovered, the quality of the recovered product, the market for it and the price that it can command and the environmental impacts of energy used by the recovery process(es).

Exercise

Let us assume that the average UK household produces 0.8 t yr⁻¹ of MSW, which contains 8% plastics, 60% of which can be recovered by separation at source and separate uplift by the collection authority (i.e. 4.8% of MSW). Let us ignore for the moment that there are at least four grades of plastics – low density polyethylene, high density polyethylene, PVC (polyvinyl chloride), PET (polyethyleneterephthalate) – in common domestic use. Our 4.8% of mixed dense plastics waste commands £50 per tonne on a good day. What is the cash value of one year's plastic recycling from our average household?

Answer

$\dfrac{0.8 \times 4.8}{100} \times 50 = £1.92$ per year per household

---

We can do similar sums for the other components in MSW that are deemed to be recyclable, namely glass, ferrous metals, aluminium cans and paper. These show that there is less than (an optimistic) £10 worth of marketable waste materials in the average household's waste over a year, including our high value plastics. The price for paper is zero to negative – i.e. charges can be made for its collection.

Recycling can be an act of faith for dedicated practitioners, but if wholesale recycling for the population at large is to be practised with (say) kerbside collection of recyclables, we need to look closely at the costs. In other words, we need to examine the value of the materials reclaimed against the extra costs incurred in collecting them, instead of just emptying the dustbin straight into the collection vehicle. If the costs of the recyclables collections are two or three times that of just emptying the bins, questions could be asked as to whether the extra resources used up by separate collection could not be put to better use (e.g. roads, hospitals, schools, old people's homes).

However, there is every indication from large-scale experimental schemes that the costs of recycling are extremely high. Table 20 gives the costs from UK experimental collection schemes (Prosser, 1991). Costs are in fact being reduced, but they still in the main greatly exceed mixed waste collection costs. There is always the possibility that costs can be reduced, e.g. by employing fortnightly waste collection schemes instead of weekly ones, as has been proposed by several local authorities. But this carries possible health implications as food wastes 'pong' in summer after two to three days.

Table 20 *UK experimental collection schemes*

Method used	Number of properties where waste is reclaimed	Reclaimed amounts (kg per household per week)	Collection participation rate (%)	Collection costs (gross) (£ per tonne)
Box at kerbside with glass, plastics, etc. separated out				
Sheffield	3050	2.3	90	140
Milton Keynes	3400	3.5	82	130
Wheeled bin				
Bury	7000	4.1	n.a.	100
Leeds	4000	n.a.	48–72	n.a.
Bottle bank				
Sutton	66 000	0.44 (glass)	n.a.	35

Source: H.J. Prosser of Warren Spring Laboratory (Institute of Wastes Management Recycling Symposium, London 14 February 1991).

Note: Proponents of separate collection claim that these costs can be halved.

Prosser further comments:

'…experience in northern America, supported by the current trials, indicates that householders will separate their waste provided that they see the materials being recycled. There have been considerable problems in finding markets for paper in North America, and large quantities are now exported. (The UK receives North American waste paper.) Collection costs are the main barrier to expansion of the source segregation schemes. While costs per tonne of reclaimed material are high, it is necessary to take account of savings in disposal costs, consisting of avoided collection, transfer and landfill costs, which may currently amount to about £20 per tonne. The Department of the Environment is currently studying possible ways to credit recycling operations with savings in disposal costs. The value of the reclaimed materials varies considerably but currently may be in the range of £25–£40 per tonne; net costs will accordingly be in the range £40–£95 per tonne.'

(Prosser, 1991)

In other words, these separate collection schemes may cost a lot of money. It is perhaps worth asking whether it is worth diverting considerable sums of money into materials recovery when other methods might be more cost effective: for example, waste minimisation or incineration with energy recovery, which helps conserve scarce energy resources.

We shall come back to this provocative thought later. Let us now examine some MSW components and their recyclability, but before we do so please read the **recycling** entry in the set book.

Which part of the recycling range of options are we considering in Section 7?

Direct recycling, i.e. materials recovery.

SAQ 27

Complete Table 21 to obtain the revenue potential per household per year (column e) on the basis of mass produced (column a), the estimated clean fraction (column b), and the possible merchant price per tonne (column d). Which are the main revenue-producing components?

Recycling
- 3 classes
Reuse
   eg returnable bottle
Dircet recycling
   material recovery and
   reuse for same initial purpose
   usually occurs at the factories
   with off cuts etc
Indirect recycling
eg. glass bottles become road surface
plastic containers become
                    fence posts.
district heating from
   incineration with heat recovery

Table 21   *Matrix for evaluating the potential revenue available in MSW components*

	Weight/ (kg per house per year)	Estimated 'clean' fraction/%	Clean weight/ (kg per house per year)	Possible merchant price (£ per tonne)	Revenue potential per household per year (£)
	a	b	c: (a × b)/100	d	e
Paper	200	60	*120*	5	$\frac{120}{1000} \times 5 = 0.6$
Plastic film	24	60		30	*0.43*
Dense plastic	18	70		60	*0.76*
Textiles	24	50		10	*0.12*
Glass	60	90		30	*1.62*
Ferrous metal	42	80		10	*0.34*
Aluminium	4	70		400	*1.12*
Total					*4.99*

(handwritten note above d column header: 1000kg)

Glass/Aluminium 55% of total income

SAQ 28

Summarise (from the set book) how recycling might be encouraged.

see answer for notes

7.2   *Paper recovery*

The UK in 1991 used 9.3 million tonnes of paper and board. The UK production portion was 4.49 million tonnes of which 3 million tonnes came from recycled paper. This is very good going indeed. However, when the recycled paper statistics are examined, it is found that 2.7 million tonnes came from the industrial sector and only 0.3 million tonnes from the domestic sector.

In fact, the waste paper market was in the doldrums and you couldn't even give the stuff away. In some instances you might have had to pay to have it collected, as the extract from the *Institute of Wastes Management Journal* shows:

Paper and skip charges 'less than for landfill'

'Oversupply from Europe and North America, and continental subsidies, are blamed for pushing British waste paper prices down to a point where the industry must charge for collected material and for the containers supplied. A statement by the UK Waste Paper Industry Committee (UKWPIC) says that current collection and processing costs of around £30 per tonne 'will rise considerably' when the Duty of Care and Carriage of Wastes provisions embodied in the Environmental Protection Act are implemented.

'Some foreign governments have reacted to the difficulties created by excessive waste paper supplies and brought in subsidies,' says Committee member Tony Abram, director of John W. Hannay and Co., one of Scotland's major recycling companies. 'As yet the British Government has not taken this initiative and we remain at a disadvantage. We are obviously concerned that some clients may have difficulty accepting the idea of a fee, but they should realise that to have waste uplifted by companies who remove it to landfill sites would still be considerably more expensive.'

Mr. Abram believes that most firms are sufficiently environmentally aware to continue to support paper recycling in spite of these charges.

High-grade waste paper has not escaped the severe reductions in pulp prices due to overproduction. UKWPIC also accepts that returns from paper collections for charities are now hardly worth the effort.'

(Institute of Wastes Management Journal, February 1991)

Another article on this topic was in the same issue of the journal.

Lost opportunities

'A loss of £4.64 on every tonne of paper collected is reported by CROP, the Milton Keynes Community Recycling Opportunities Programme. In order to stay in the market it must now separate magazines from newspapers, trebling the time taken to unload a collection vehicle.

In an attempt to strike a balance between efficient commercial operation and benefit to the environment, CROP general manager Simon Leadbeater, appointed last November, has launched a membership scheme with annual subscriptions ranging from £2 for Juniors to £50 for Life members.'

(Institute of Wastes Management Journal, February 1991)

Even one of the best planned schemes, such as the CROP scheme in Milton Keynes, reports a loss on waste paper.

The current 'hope' is that two planned waste paper mills at Gartcosh and Aylesford taking $200\,000$ t yr^{-1} will jointly expand waste paper intake by $400\,000$ t yr^{-1} at a cost of over £400 million. (To put this in context, a $400\,000$ t yr^{-1} MSW incinerator for Hampshire with energy recovery and power generation could cost about £70 million.)

There are 11 basic grades of waste paper ranging from Group 1 (best white shavings) to Group 11 (contaminated grades). The best grades command reasonable prices. Newsprint and periodicals can cost money for uplift (£5 per tonne as at August 1992).

The future for large-scale paper recovery from MSW, as opposed to the better grades from the specialised trade sources, does not look promising. The domestic waste paper market also has to compete with imports at very low prices.

from Europe & US

7.3   Bottles

SAQ 29

From the **bottle** entry and on the basis of the figures in Figures 8 and 9 in the set book:

(a) Calculate the total energy used for 10 trips by refillable bottle.   *9 kWh_e*

(b) Calculate the total energy used for 10 non-refillable bottles.   *19 kWh_e*

(c) What are the energy savings for (b) compared with (a)?   *10 kWh_e*

(d) Assuming that it now requires 30% less energy to manufacture non-refillable bottles, recalculate (b).   *15.7 kWh_e*

(e) What is the energy expenditure?   *6.7 kWh_e*

SAQ 29 shows that refillable bottles can save energy. However, it is often stated by trade sources that they must be transported long distances for refilling and that this might cancel out the energy savings. The sad fact is that the UK consumer's choice of returnable refillable bottles in supermarkets is virtually zero compared with French, German, Swedish, Danish, Dutch, Norwegian and Finnish supermarkets. So what is to be done?

Well, the only other choices are separation at source and kerbside collection (very expensive) or taking them to the bottle bank (hopefully on the same shopping trip, otherwise the fuel used if going by car may negate the energy saved by the bottle manufacturer).

Let's examine the UK's performance.

The UK melts 2.8 million t yr^{-1} of glass of which 1.8 m t yr^{-1} is used for glass containers (Glass Manufacturers Federation). That is a lot of glass to throw away. The statistics for glass recycling in 1990 (trade and domestic figures combined) show that 370 000 tonnes of glass were recycled in 1990, which means that a claimed 20% of glass overall is recycled. However, Germany and Holland can manage recycling rates approaching 60%, so we (and they) could do better! The glass industry is actively working to increase recycling rates and intensifying public education on the merits of using bottle banks.

What is the glass industry doing?

Expanding the bottle bank system.

Paying stable prices for glass at the factory gate.

Encouraging good quality collection systems.

Encouraging 'bring' recycling systems at local authority level.

Intensifying public education.

However, let us not forget that returnable, refillable bottles save energy. Other countries make the returnable system work (Sweden, Norway, France and 12 states in the USA do it). Read the **bottle bill** entry in the set book.

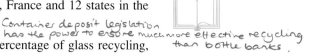

Container deposit legislation has the power to ensure much more effective recycling than bottle banks.

Table 22 shows that although the UK has a respectable percentage of glass recycling, other EC countries have done much better.

Table 22   *Percentages of glass recycled in EC countries*

Netherlands	66
Belgium	60
Germany	54
Italy	50
France	45
Denmark	40
Portugal	30
Spain	27
UK	21
Eire	18
Greece	16

Source: House of Commons Written Answers, 18 June 1991, Col. 129.

7.4   Cans

There are two types of can in use in the UK: coated steel and aluminium. The former is used by approximately half the soft drinks market and nearly all the food and pet food market. Aluminium cans are used by the other half of the soft drinks market. The can types are in strong competition with each other for markets.

Steel can be put in the dustbin and magnetically extracted or, as TV 3 shows, magnetically extracted from the incinerator bottom ash. Aluminium, being non-magnetic, may be taken to a 'Cash a Can Bank' where (say) 1p per can is raised for charity.

We can expect the recycling efforts for both aluminium and steel cans to be expanded considerably over the next few years under the impetus of EC legislation and 'green' marketing ventures. However, the recycling of steel and aluminium cans in the UK has a long way to go to achieve the US recycling rate in 1989 of 63.6% for aluminium cans (the UK 1992 rate was 16%). Sweden achieves a greater than 90% recycling rate for aluminium cans. This is greatly helped by mandatory deposits.

There is really not a lot to say about metals recycling. Ferrous metals can be readily extracted from MSW and should be extracted in all large urban conurbations. Greater Manchester has installed its third magnetic extraction unit at Salford and expects to reclaim 80 million steel cans annually from Salford's MSW. This provides scrap steel for remelting, which is much more energy efficient than mining and smelting iron ore to make steel, but also provides some marginal savings in MSW disposal costs. Remember that about 95% by mass of the MSW will remain for disposal and that all those trucks, transfer stations, etc., have been bought and have to be run and paid for, so marginal reductions in waste throughput do not bring proportional savings owing to the high fixed costs..

The US can manufacturers' promotional literature (1990) gave the following 'recycling fun facts':

How Much Can Your Group Make?

'Your group can earn:

$100

$500

$ 1000

$10 000

Example:

1   Twenty volunteers agree to 'round up' 20 households apiece to save cans.

2   Twenty times 20 homes = 400 households.

3   Each household saves 50 cans a month.

4   Total: 20 000 cans a month at 2 cents per can.

5   Value: about $250* at today's scrap prices.

6   Annual income: $3000.*

*These figures are based on a nationwide average of $35 per lb. Market prices for used beverage cans vary considerably from time to time in various areas of the country.'

(from US Can Manufacturers Institute, 1990)

What is also interesting from the US promotional literature aimed at charities (and is an example to us all) is the example of what a group can earn at 2 cents per can:

More Recycling Fun Facts

'Recycling saves 95% of the energy required to make aluminium from ore.

In 1988, aluminium companies saved the energy equivalent of over 10 million barrels of oil or 60 billion kilowatt hours. This represents enough energy to supply the electrical needs of a city the size of Pittsburgh for about six years.

Fifty-three million pounds of aluminium were recycled in 1972. Today we exceed that amount every two weeks.

Some 55 000 cans are recycled every minute nationwide.

Used aluminium cans that are recycled are returned to store shelves within 6 weeks.

In 1968, there were only 8 different beverages sold in aluminium cans – 3 soft drinks and 5 brands of beer. Today more than 95% of all canned beer and soft drinks are sold in aluminium cans.

Twenty years ago, one pound of aluminium made 19 12-ounce cans. By continuing to develop new technologies to reduce the can's weight, the industry now produces an average of 28 cans from every pound of aluminium.'

(from US Can Manufacturers Institute, 1990)

7.5   *Plastics*

Read the *plastics* related entries in the set book, paying special attention to the *plastics recycling* entry. Now attempt SAQ 30. And read the *polyvinyl chloride* entry before trying SAQ 31.

SAQ 30

Summarise the problems associated with the recycling of plastics in MSW. How have the French overcome these problems with respect to PVC bottles? (Refer to set book Figure 69).

See answer for notes

SAQ 31

Summarise the manufacturing energy requirements for PVC, and the subsequent case for the disposal of plastics by incineration with energy recovery.

PVC is less energy intensive to produce than other plastics.

Plastic in MSW raises the CV considerably. So incineration with energy recovery is effective. It produces a denser ash than standard MSW — less compaction needed on landfilling. 90% volume reduction achieved by incineration.

Plastics are often unfairly projected as bêtes noires in recycling discussions. As the first part of this text showed, their selective use can save energy and produce less waste. Their problem (and their advantage) is longevity and consequent high profile as litter. However, when all energy aspects are considered (and remember energy is a resource too) there is a case to be made for the use of plastics. Their recycling (along with other MSW components) can be solved by segregation at source (very costly) or by secondary products manufacture from mixed plastics (e.g. bin liners) or by incineration with energy recovery to recover their indigenous energy content. This is the preferred route by the plastics industry for the mixed plastic components in household waste. To send the current volume of plastics to landfill that we do is patently absurd. They occupy proportionately greater space than the cans, bottles, papers and putrescible content of MSW and do not degrade nor necessarily stabilise in the landfill site.

7.6   *Summary*

Materials recovery from domestic waste is not easy to do. It requires action by the householder to separate the waste and either put it out for collection (very costly) or take to special bottle or paper banks (the 'bring' system). Alternatively, it needs expensive separation processes (e.g. WDF production) coupled with materials recovery.

There are clear market constraints for waste paper and quality constraints for virgin plastics manufacture. Metal cans and glass bottles do have an advantage of being easily remelted and reformed. However, the overall energy and environmental balance of one form of packaging over another needs careful consideration. Ease of recycling can be helped by designing for it at the manufacturing stage.

We should not forget that the case for recycling (as far as the government and and hard-pressed local authorities are concerned) rests on economics. This is brought out in SAQ 32 which shows the crucial role that disposal costs play in determining the viability of recycling.

SAQ 32

Figure 22 shows a 'sensitivity graph' for the net cost per tonne of recyclables plotted against change in cost factor relative to base case (value 1.0).

(a)   What is the net cost per tonne of recyclables at cost factor 1?

(b)   What is the net cost per tonne if the disposal cost rises to £30 t^{-1}?

(c)   What revenue per tonne of recyclables is built into Figure 22?

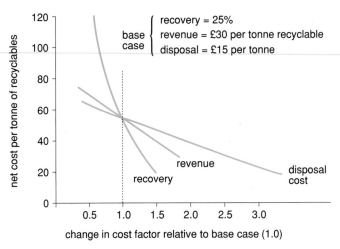

Figure 22   *Sensitivity graph for net cost per tonne of recyclables recovered from household waste vs change in cost factor.*

8 WASTE MINIMISATION AND RESOURCE CONSERVATION POLICIES

8.1 Possibilities for minimisation

We must conclude the MSW component of the wastes management block with a brief discussion on *waste minimisation* (section (vii) under *wastes*). This can mean many things to many people. For example, the chemical industry's guidelines on waste minimisation as outlined in the set book include 'design for maximum energy efficiency', and 'make minimum use of process water'. But what does waste minimisation mean to *you*?

On the basis of your household waste survey, what could you minimise or cut back on? My list includes:

1   buying one Sunday newspaper instead of two (I don't need the colour magazines, selling for the most part expensive holidays, cars, dresses or cigarettes, either, but there is no opt-out route on this one);

2   more reuse of plastic carrier bags;

3   even more composting of household vegetable wastes (but not foodstuffs because of potential vermin problems);

4   buying larger and or refillable containers of concentrated washing-up liquid;

5   trying to compost newspapers (difficult one this);

6   persevering with potentially energy-wasting trips to the bottle bank by storing up more bottles to make the trip worthwhile (my nearest one is over one and a half miles away, i.e. a three mile round trip).

The boxed text gives an industrial example of what the 3M Company achieved in eliminating ammonium sulphate discharges at its Chemolite Center in Cottage Grove, Minnesota, USA.

Problem

A 3M Chemolite Center plant in Cottage Grove, Minnesota, makes magnetic oxides for recording products. Ammonium sulphate, a by-product of the process, was being discharged to the wastewater treatment facility that serves the entire Chemolite complex. It passed through that system virtually untreated and went into the river. Being mixed with millions of gallons of other waste water diluted the ammonium sulphate so much there was no practical method to remove or recover it there. State regulations, however, required a reduction of ammonia from the Chemolite effluent.

Solution

3M decided to 'go after' the ammonium sulphate before it could get diluted in the process waste stream. After studying various processes for ammonium sulphate removal and recovery, vapour compression evaporation was settled on as the most applicable technology. This means that the vapour is compressed (just like air in a bike pump) with a subsequent increase in temperature which enables it to be reused as a heating medium for evaporation purposes. This enabled the ammonium sulphate to be concentrated to a 40% solution, upgraded to commercial quality farm fertiliser and sold.

3M kept federal and state environmental authorities informed at all stages of the Chemolite project.

Payoff

• The need for pollution control equipment was eliminated, saving $1 million. Cost of the vapour compression evaporator was $1.5 million.

• Fertiliser sales produced annual revenues of $150 000.

• 677 tons of water pollution were prevented annually.

Other examples are covered in the ***pollution prevention pays*** entry in the set book. You will also see examples of paper recycling and waste minimisation in the second television programme (TV 4) and the broadcast notes.

8.2   *Packaging waste reduction*

Packaging (depending on how it's defined) constitutes a major proportion of MSW, and the packaging industry has not been backward in doing its bit to reduce the quantities used and in assisting recyclability too, where practicable.

Figure 23 (from the Steel Can Recycling Information Bureau) gives one example of packaging reduction for the 33-cl beverage can.

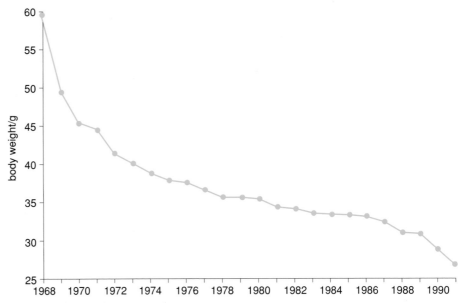

Figure 23   *Steel can body weight reduction for a 33-cl beverage can.*

By how much has the 33-cl can been reduced in weight between 1968 and 1990?

1990 index = 50; 1968 index = 100.

So there has been a 50% weight reduction.

Similarly, pet food cans have been reduced from 100 in 1979 to 83 in 1989; this is a 17% reduction.

As an extended example of what is involved in waste reduction, the boxed text which follows is based on Coca-Cola Foods Drink Box Environmental Profile (Coca-Cola Foods, Houston, June 1991). This is aimed at US legislation and documents Coca-Cola's attempts at waste minimisation and environmental impact reduction for its packaged orange juice products. Figures 24 to 26 also refer. Note that the energy units are in British thermal units (Btu) where 1 Btu = 1055 J, and the volumes are in US gallons where 1 US gallon = 0.8 UK gallon or 3.64 litres.

Drink Boxes create less waste than other packages

As space in landfills around the country decreases, it becomes more and more important to reduce the amount of trash we throw out.

Thanks to a unique design that combines ultra-thin layers of paper, plastic and aluminum foil, the Drink Box holds more liquid with less material than any other ready-to-drink beverage container. In fact, no other leading single-serve package is as materials efficient as the Drink Box.

Not only does this reduction in materials lighten truckloads and increase energy efficiency, but minimal packaging lightens the load on our waste disposal system.

Drink Boxes save energy and our atmosphere

Energy use, while critical in any modern society, has been the focus of environmental concern over the past decade as scientists learn more about the effect of emissions on our atmosphere.

The conclusion: reducing energy use will help save the atmosphere from emissions that have been implicated in global warming, acid rain, ozone depletion and air pollution.

From design to disposal, the Drink Box saves energy every step of the way.

Due to their lightweight design and efficient shape, aseptic packages require less energy to make, fill, sterilise, transport and store than any comparable package.

Most important, the Drink Box does not need to be refrigerated to retain the quality of its contents. Even delicate beverages like juice and milk remain good tasting for up to a year without costly and energy-intensive refrigeration or the use of artificial preservatives.

As a result, the Drink Box uses less total energy than virtually any other beverage package available today.

Drink Boxes can now be recycled

One of the best ways to keep a product from entering the waste stream is to use it again – or recycle it into something new. Because they are made primarily from paper, Drink Boxes are natural candidates for recycling.

Paper mills can reuse paper pulp separated from discarded Drink Boxes to make a variety of high-quality paper goods. The simple process, called hydrapulping, uses agitated water to separate the paper from the polyethylene and aluminium foil in Drink Boxes. While the paper fibre is used to make tissues, paper towels, cardboard and other products, the plastic and foil can be processed with mixed plastics to form a maintenance-free lumber substitute and other construction products.

Recently, the two leading manufacturers – Tetra Pak and Combibloc – initiated a joint programme to demonstrate the feasibility of collecting and recycling Drink Boxes. Used packages are being collected from kerbside programmes and/or schools in selected communities in 11 states across the country, including California, Connecticut, Illinois, Maryland, Massachusetts, Minnesota, New York, Oregon, Rhode Island, Vermont and Washington.

Drink Boxes are toxic-free

Though we all want to reduce the amount of material that ends up in a landfill, not everything can be diverted. Even recycled products, like glass bottles and aluminum cans, eventually find their way to the landfill. That's why it is so important that waste materials be free of toxic inks and dyes.

The Drink Box is made without toxic materials and is safe in landfills. Even the inks used on the Drink Box have been carefully selected to avoid heavy metals that might contribute to toxic runoff or groundwater contamination.

Drink Boxes are safe for incineration

The absence of toxics also means that discarded Drink Boxes provide a clean source of fuel for modern waste-to-energy facilities. Waste-to-energy incineration reduces the volume of garbage by as much as 90%. At the same time, combustion generates heat and steam energy that can be captured to heat homes or produce electricity.

Coca-Cola Foods and the aseptic package

At Coca-Cola Foods we are very concerned with the impact of all our packages on the environment. We are the world's leading producer of juice and juice drink products available in both ready-to-serve and frozen concentrate forms. For each product form and package size, we have selected the most efficient and environmentally sound package, given the technology available today.

The aseptic package is one of the most innovative and environmentally responsive product containers we use. The Drink Box allows us to deliver high-quality beverages with the safety and convenience consumers demand, while helping to address our national need for energy conservation and waste reduction.

So, when it comes to packaging for consumers and the environment, we believe good things really do come in small packages – the aseptic Drink Box.

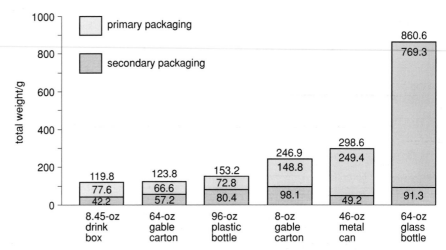

Figure 24 *Total packaging weight of various juice packages (per 64 ounces): includes package and shipping/storage containers.*

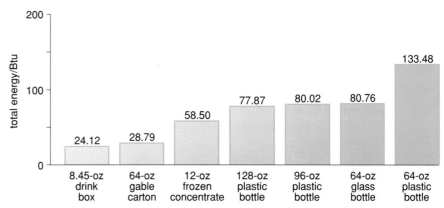

Figure 25 *Total energy use associated with various juice packages (per 1000 gallons): includes energy used in package manufacturing, filling, distribution, refrigeration and disposal.*

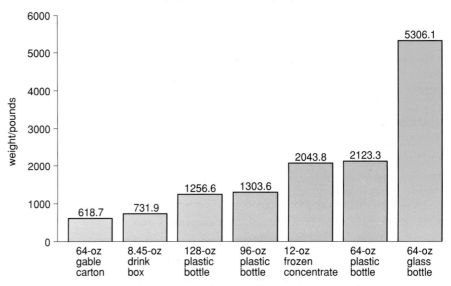

Figure 26 *Total waste produced by various juice packages (per 1000 gallons of juice delivered): includes solid waste, waste water and air emissions.*

What might you conclude from the Coca-Cola report regarding energy consumption and packaging weight *vis-à-vis* the 64-oz glass bottle?

From Figure 24, the reduction in packaging weight for 64 ounces of juice using the drink box is (860.6 − 119.8)/860.6 = 86%.

From Figure 25, the reduction in total energy use associated with 1000 gallons of juice (including refrigeration etc.) is (133.48 − 24.12)/133.48 = 82%.

SAQ 33

Using the Coca-Cola figures:

(a) What is the percentage waste reduction per 1000 gallons using the 8.45-oz drink box and the 64-oz glass bottle?

(b) Recalculate the percentage weight reduction assuming 50% of the glass bottles are recycled via bottle banks and that the 8.45-oz drink box is sent to landfill.

(c) Compare the 50% glass recycling waste value with the 64-oz plastic bottle waste (no recycling).

8.3 Resource conservation measures aimed at waste minimisation

Practical measures constitute the theme of this course, and the agenda now being set by the European Parliamentary Scientific and Technical Options Assessment Group is summarised below. Each heading could have a book to itself, but, sadly, space does not permit it. We will also meet some more of this area in Units 10 and 14–16.

Industry

> develop new technologies;
>
> manage the enterprise with the view 'no harm/low risk';
>
> change to clean technologies;
>
> renounce unnecessary and risky or harmful materials;
>
> supply data and information on products and manufacturing processes (concerning environmental impact);
>
> accept the environmental costs of a product as production costs;
>
> ensure a functioning marketing system for recyclable and recycled products.

Industrial associations

> inform their members about new technologies;
>
> inform their members about the hazards of certain substances and materials;
>
> inform their members about recycling possibilities;
>
> help their members with the environmental management of their enterprises.

Consumer associations

> help to develop an environmental labelling for products;
>
> inform about environmentally acceptable products;
>
> inform about an environmental behaviour of consumption;
>
> develop education programmes for environmental behaviour.

Politics

> direct the waste production with legal instruments;
>
> direct the waste production with economic instruments;
>
> develop promotion programmes for waste prevention;
>
> develop a waste prevention and recovery infrastructure;
>
> represent a model for waste conscient behaviour.

Administration

> shorten the time span needed for the approval of new facilities which produce less waste than the old ones;
>
> control the waste production of existing manufacturing plants;
>
> help the enterprises to find a way to environmental management;
>
> support the enforcement of the required infrastructure.

General public

> direct the waste production by determined consumption behaviour;
>
> renounce products with useless packaging material;
>
> prefer products that cause less waste;
>
> prefer products that create less waste during production ;
>
> renounce unnecessary products;
>
> inform the neighbour about the environmental quality of the product;
>
> separate recoverable products and materials.

As examples of some of these measures, design for recycling and eco-labelling are discussed next.

8.3.1   Design for recycling

To take a few common examples, one plastic bottle made out of two different polymers plus a metal cap, or cans produced from two or three different metals makes recycling nonsense. We can learn from Sweden again, where most cans are of aluminium and the recovery rate is 90% of production through the use of reverse vending machines.

Similarly the incorporation of ever more plastics, alloys and fancy trims in motor cars inhibits the reclamation of materials when they reach the end of their useful life. I would favour a car recycling deposit at the time of first purchase which is only redeemable at licensed vehicle dismantlers. This would ensure that (a) vehicles are returned, (b) vehicles are dismantled and recycled in authorised locations by approved methods, and not at any backstreet location, and (c) components are either reclaimed for refurbishment or materials recovery. Figure 27 shows the complexity of the task and why plastics manufacturers are now standardising plastics grades in order to assist materials recovery. The onus could also be placed on the vehicle manufacturers to design for recycle through a variable deposit. It is quite conceivable that a virtually all-metal Mercedes could carry a smaller deposit than the confection of alloys, metals and plastics that is used in many small cars today. On a car-related topic, there should also be a substantial refundable deposit on lead-acid batteries so that all batteries eventually end up at authorised recycling centres. The potential for environmental insult, injury and/or health problems from the unauthorised disposal or burning of casings of lead-acid batteries and disposal of acid liquors and sludges can thereby be eliminated. Similarly, a deposit on mercury or cadmium batteries redeemable at points of sale could do much to restrict their indiscriminate disposal in the MSW stream. As noted in Section 2.1, the British Battery Manufacturers Association are initiating collection schemes for selected types of batteries, but they are not in favour of collecting all used batteries since the amounts of mercury, cadmium, lead and other potentially harmful materials used in batteries which fall outside the scope of the directive are too small to be of environmental significance and are generally of too low a value to make recycling an economic proposition.

8.3.2   Eco-labelling for consumer information

This should begin with a recycling statement being provided on all packaging which indicates (a) what resources have been used to provide the packaging and (b) what can be saved if it is recycled for materials recovery or reused if it is a refillable reusable container. Some products should be labelled as environmentally dangerous, such as mercury or cadmium batteries and aerosol canisters with chlorofluorocarbon propellants, so that consumers may make an informed choice.

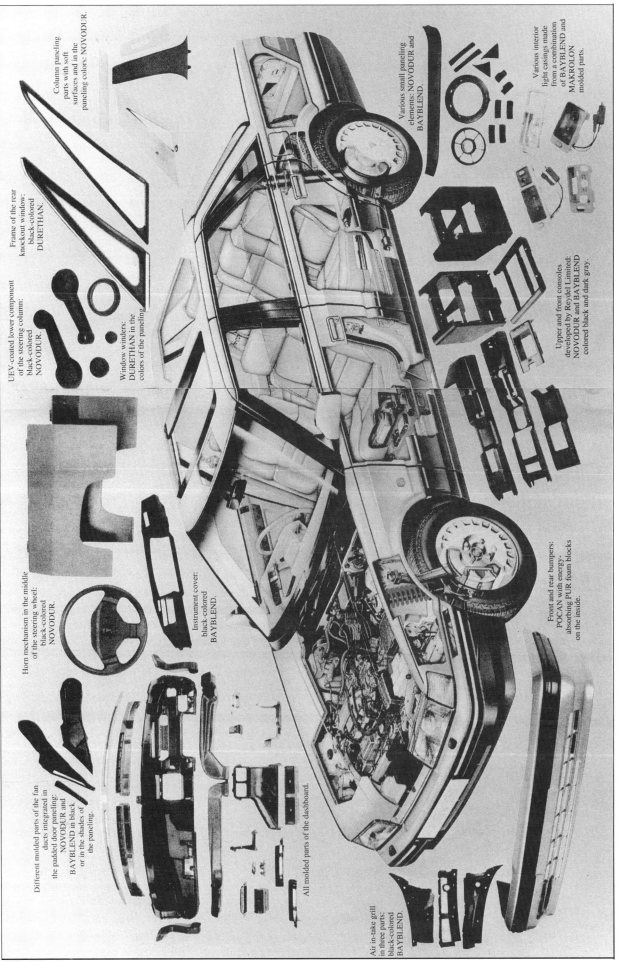

Figure 27   *Exploded view of car body showing the various plastics components commonly used and their commercial specification.*

The National Advisory Group on Eco-Labelling has stated:

> 'The European Commission has now published its proposals for a draft Council Regulation for an EC eco-labelling scheme. The draft Regulation enables a Community-wide scheme to be established at the earliest opportunity, in the same manner in all Member States, without any delay or difference resulting from transposition into national law. The benefit of the Community scheme will be in uniformity of products bearing the eco-label very much in accord with the creation of the single market.'

This means that life-cycle or cradle-to-grave assessment is needed, i.e. a product's effect on the environment should be examined at all stages from the raw materials used in its manufacture, production, distribution and use to its disposal. The EC proposal will utilise the assessment format shown in Table 23 to draw up specific criteria for each product group.

Table 23   *Eco-labelling matrix*

Environmental field	Product life cycle				
	Pre-production	Production	Distribution (including packaging)	Utilisation	Disposal
Waste relevance					
Soil pollution and degradation					
Water contamination					
Air contamination					
Noise					
Consumption of energy					
Consumption of natural resources					
Effect on ecosystems					

environmental
audits
– an account by
manufacturers of
products produced
and processes,
and their effect on
environment

As well as eco-labelling, we can also expect ***environmental audits*** to appear on the scene. There is a huge variety of environmental audits. These range from compliance audit, which checks that the company is doing the minimum required by law, to a complete assessment of a plant's environmental impact and how it can be reduced by improvements to plant design and procedures. The Coca-Cola drink box statement discussed in Section 8.2 is a good example of what may be required in the future.

The European Commission's draft proposal published in February 1991 was for a comprehensive management tool, covering products from the cradle to the grave. It considered the minimisation of waste, the use of natural resources, energy choice and the reduction of its use, packaging, transportation, accident prevention, compliance with the law, and company policy. (But, following protests from some member states, audits will not be made mandatory.)

Under EC guidelines, if an audit is completed companies have to draw up an environmental statement (a summary of the audit, again covered by specific guidelines) for public consultation on request. This statement would have to be registered with a competent authority established by the member states.

The waste industry is already required to prepare an environmental statement for any incineration plant greater than 1 t hr^{-1} (or landfill site in excess of 75 000 t yr^{-1}) as set out in circular EC/15/88 and Statutory Instrument 1199, and the Town and County Planning (Assessment of Environmental Effects) Regulations 1988. The statement must accompany the application for planning permission for the proposed development. MSW and hazardous waste incineration falls within the listed

Schedule 1 projects where an environmental assessment is required in all cases. (It makes good sense anyway.)

8.4   *Concluding remarks*

In Units 8–9 we have examined the requirements of the EPA and the total dominance of landfill in the UK's management strategy for MSW (and industrial wastes). This massive UK bias towards one particular disposal method has undoubtedly militated against both recycling for materials recovery and incineration with energy recovery. However, there is a rising tide of awareness of recycling possibilities, plus the threat of action to enforce more recycling by the EC, to engender the hope that more will be done. Her Majesty's Government have a public commitment to 25% recycling of MSW by the year 2000. Let us hope that this will indeed come about. We must, however, be mindful of the statement by Barton and Prosser.

> '…any system taken beyond certain limits will result not only in unjustifiable financial costs but can also become a net user of the very 'resources' it is designed to conserve.'
>
> *(Barton and Prosser, 1990)*

We are not yet in this position in the UK. As this part of the course has shown, there is scope for much greater recycling of *selected* materials in MSW.

Barton and Prosser have also commented:

> 'However, the improvements in economic incentive do not change the basic problem, i.e. recycling is a complex chain which has proved, time and again, to be fragile in terms of maintaining production capacity to utilise the scrap and establishing markets for products made. Not only does capacity take time to develop when requirements are known, for some recyclables from domestic waste, we don't yet have a clear picture of what those requirements are. Given that it is local authorities' and the waste management industries' prime task to ensure safe disposal, it is unrealistic and unsound to implement collection systems without a thorough evaluation of demand for each commodity and a recognition that revenues will at times be uncertain, possibly non-existent. However, local authorities and the waste management industry can create and promote a strong and increasing demand for products containing recycled materials both directly and through influencing the public and local businesses. In addition they can implement waste management techniques which facilitate maintaining collection infrastructure for recyclables, developing non-dumping options when demand falls and implementing 'closed loop' recycling options such as composting.
>
> Actions speak louder than words and the commodity industries' confidence in the local authority and waste management industry to play their full part has not been helped by the almost total reliance of landfilling, however soundly based selection of this option may have been in the past.'
>
> *(Barton and Prosser, 1990)*

SAQ 34

Make a generic list of common hazardous household products under the headings of corrosive, flammable, toxic and reactive.

SAQ 35

Under the respective headings of (1) reduce, (2) reuse, (3) recycle, (4) disposal, for common household items, what steps would you take to minimise the use and/or impact of 'hazardous' household products? Note that 'hazardous', embraces toxicity, irritants, flammability, reactivity, corrosiveness, asphyxiation, damage to the water, air, land, living organisms.

SAQs 34 and 35 should start you thinking about the next component of the wastes management block: hazardous wastes management.

References

BARTON, J. R. AND PROSSER, H. (1990) Institute of Wastes Management and Department of the Environment Joint Conference on Recycling, London, 4 December 1990

BEVAN, R. E. (1967) *Notes on the Science and Practice of the Controlled Tipping of Refuse*, Institute of Solid Waste Management.

DEPARTMENT OF THE ENVIRONMENT/WELSH OFFICE (1976) *The Balancing of Interests between Water Protection and Waste Disposal*, DoE Circular no. 39/76.

HIGGINSON, A. E. (1982) *The Analysis of Domestic Waste*, Institute of Wastes Management.

MARPLES, A. (1990) Summary paper presented to the Institute of Wastes Management on 12 December 1990, Bury St. Edmunds.

PORTEOUS, A. (1992) *Dictionary of Environmental Science and Technology*, John Wiley & Sons (T237 set book).

PROSSER, H. J. (1991) Institute of Wastes Management Recycling Symposium, London, 14 February 1991.

SKITT, J. (1979) *Waste Disposal, Management and Practice*, Knight.

TAYLOR, R. (1989) 'The true cost of landfill – energy recycling is strong competitor', *Warmer Bulletin*, Summer 1989 (see Appendix 3).

VOGG, H. *et al.* (1986) 'The specific role of cadmium and mercury in municipal solid waste incineration', *Waste Management and Research*, 4(1), March 1986.

Acknowledgements

Grateful acknowledgement is made to the following sources for permission to reproduce material in this unit.

Text

pp. 8–9: From *The Guardian*, 20 September 1991; *pp. 31–32:* 'Veto on quarry dump scheme', *Northamptonshire Evening Telegraph*, 1st December 1982; *pp. 65–6:* 'Paper and skip charges 'less than for landfill'', and 'Lost opportunities', *Institute of Wastes Management Journal*, February 1991, Institute of Wastes Management; *p. 73: The Drink Box – An Environmental Profile of An Innovative Package*, courtesy of Coca-Cola Foods; Barton, J. R. and Prosser, H. (1990) Conference On Recycling, Institute of Wastes Management; *Appendix 3:* Taylor, R. (1989) 'The true cost of landfill – energy recycling is strong competitor, *Warmer Bulletin*, Summer 1989, The Warmer Campaign.

Figures

Cover illustration: Based on an original by Ian Howatson, courtesy of Ian Howatson Illustration, Buckingham; *cover photograph:* Shanks & McEwan (Waste Services) Ltd; *Figure 1:* From the *Report of the Non-Statutory Public Enquiry into the Gas Explosion at Loscoe, Derbyshire* (1986) courtesy of Derbyshire County Council; *Figures 3 & 4:* From *The Can Makers Report 1991*, courtesy of The Can Makers Ltd; *Figure 7:* adapted from *The Conference On Leachate Management In Landfill*, courtesy of the Institute of Wastes Management; *Figures 9, 10, 11:* courtesy of the Waste Disposal Operations Division, Somerset County Council; *Figures 12, 13, 14:* Bevan, R. E. (1967) *Science and Practice of Controlled Tipping*, Institute of Wastes Management; *Figure 20:* Gray, K. R. (1972) *Waste Disposal Management and Practice*, Charles Knight; *Figure 23:* Courtesy of British Steel Tinplate; *Figures 24, 25, 26:* From *The Drink Box – An Environmental Profile of An Innovative Package*, courtesy of Coca-Cola Foods; *Figure 27:* From *Bayer Magazine – Bayer and Rover. Right From The Start*, courtesy of Bayer UK plc.

Tables

Tables 1, 4, 5: From *Waste Disposal Statistics*, Courtesy of The Chartered Institute of Public Finance & Accountancy; *Table 2:* Kin Ho, T. (1982) Ph.D. Thesis, University of Stirling; *Table 3:* Townend, W. K. (1990) 'The impact of goods packaging on household waste', *Waste Management*, February 1990, Institute of Wastes Management; *Table 6:* Barton, J. (1991) 'Resource conservation v pollution control', *Wastes Management*, September 1991, © Warren Spring Laboratory, Stevenage/Crown Copyright; *Table 7:* Marchant, A. N. (1982) 'Landfill gas analysis', *The Sweet Smell of Success*, IWM Spring Meeting, 18 March 1982, Institute of Wastes Management; *Tables 12 & 13:* Reprinted by permission of the Council of the Institution of Mechanical Engineers from McKinley, W. 'Incineration, Past and Future', seminar, 13 December 1989/Deutsche Babcock Anlagen A.G., Parkstrasse 29, D 4150 Krefeld 11, Germany; *Table 18:* Courtesy of Urban Waste and Power, Ashford, Kent.

APPENDIX 1   WASTE ON LAND
SECTION TITLES OF THE
ENVIRONMENTAL PROTECTION ACT

Preliminary

29 Preliminary

30 Authorities for purposes of this part

31 Power to create regional authorities for purposes of waste regulation

32 Transition to waste disposal companies etc.

Prohibition on unauthorised or harmful depositing, treatment or disposal of waste

33 Prohibition on unauthorised or harmful deposit, treatment or disposal etc. of waste.

34 Duty of care etc. as respects waste.

Waste management licences

35 Waste management licences: general

36 Grant of licences

37 Variation of licences

38 Revocation and suspension of licences

39 Surrender of licences

40 Transfer of licences

41 Fees and charges for licences

42 Supervision of licensed activities

43 Appeals to Secretary of State from decisions with respect to licences

44 Offences of making false statements.

Collection, disposal or treatment of controlled waste

45 Collection of controlled waste

46 Receptacles for household waste

47 Receptacles for commercial or industrial waste

48 Duties of waste collection authorities as respects disposal of waste collected

49 Waste recycling plans by collection authorities

50 Waste disposal plans of waste regulation authorities

51 Functions of waste disposal authorities

52 Payments for recycling and disposal etc. of waste

53 Duties of authorities as respects disposal of waste collected: Scotland

54 Special provisions for land occupied by disposal authorities: Scotland

55 Powers for recycling waste

56 Powers for recycling waste: Scotland

57 Power of Secretary of State to require waste to be accepted, treated, disposed of or delivered.

58 Power of Secretary of State to require waste to be accepted, treated, disposed of or delivered: Scotland.

59 Powers to require removal of waste unlawfully deposited

60 Interference with waste sites and receptacles for waste

61 Duty of waste regulation authorities as respects closed landfills

APPENDIX 2
WASTE MANAGEMENT PAPERS
(DEPARTMENT OF THE ENVIRONMENT)

1   Reclamation, Treatment and Disposal of Wastes – An Evaluation of Options, HMSO 1976

2   Waste Disposal Surveys, HMSO 1976

3   Guidelines for the Preparation of a Waste Disposal Plan, HMSO 1976.

4   The Licensing of Waste Disposal Sites, HMSO 1976. (Also see The Licensing of Waste Facilities: a Revision of Waste Management, Paper 4, HMSO 1988).

5   The Relationship between Waste Disposal Authorities and Private Industry, HMSO 1976.

6   Polychlorinated Biphenyl (PCB) Wastes – A Technical Memorandum on Reclamation, Treatment and Disposal Including a Code of Practice, HMSO 1976.

7   Mineral Oil Wastes – A Technical Memorandum on Arisings, Treatment and Disposal Including a Code of Practice, HMSO 1976.

8   Heat-treatment Cyanide Wastes – A Technical Memorandum on Arisings, Treatment and Disposal Including a Code of Practice, HMSO 1976.

9   Halogenated Hydrocarbon Solvent Wastes from Cleaning Processes – A Technical Memorandum on Reclamation and Disposal Including a Code of Practice, HMSO 1976.

10   Local Authority Waste Disposal Statistics 1974/75, HMSO 1976.

11   Metal Finishing Wastes – A Technical Memorandum on Arisings, Treatment and Disposal Including a Code of Practice, HMSO 1976.

12   Mercury Bearing Wastes – A Technical Memorandum on Storage, Handling, Treatment and Recovery of Mercury Including a Code of Practice, HMSO 1977.

13   Tarry and Distillation Wastes and Other Chemical Based Residues – A Technical Memorandum on Arisings, Treatment and Disposal Including a Code of Practice, HMSO 1977.

14   Solvent Wastes (excluding Halogenated Hydrocarbons) – A Technical Memorandum on Reclamation and Disposal Including a Code of Practice, HMSO 1977.

15   Halogenated Organic Wastes – A Technical Memorandum on Arisings, Treatment and Disposal Including a Code of Practice, HMSO 1978.

16   Wood Preserving Wastes – A Technical Memorandum on Arisings, Treatment and Disposal Including a Code of Practice, HMSO 1978.

17   Wastes from Tanning, Leather Dressing and Fellmongering – A Technical Memorandum on Recovery, Treatment and Disposal Including a Code of Practice, HMSO 1978

18   Asbestos Wastes: A Technical Memorandum on Arisings and Disposal Including a Code of Practice, HMSO 1978.

19   Wastes from the Manufacture of Pharmaceuticals, Toiletries and Cosmetics – A Technical Memorandum on Arisings, Treatment and Disposal Including a Code of Practice, HMSO 1978.

20   Arsenic-bearing Wastes: A Technical Memorandum on Recovery, Treatment and Disposal, Including a Code of Practice, HMSO 1980.

21   Pesticide Wastes: a Technical Memorandum on Arisings and Disposal Including a Code of Practice, HMSO 1980.

22   Local Authority Waste Disposal Statistics, 1974–75 to 1977–78: Second Analysis of Annual Returns from English Waste Disposal Authorities, HMSO 1980.

23   Special Wastes: a Technical Memorandum on Arisings, Treatment and Disposal,

Including a Code of Practice, HMSO 1983.

25   Clinical Wastes: a Technical Memorandum on Arisings, Treatment and Disposal, Including a Code of Practice, HMSO 1983.

26   Landfilling Wastes: a Technical Memorandum for the Disposal of Wastes on Landfill Sites, HMSO 1986.

27   The Control of Landfill Gas: a Technical Memorandum on the Monitoring and Control of Landfill Gas, HMSO 1989.

28   Recycling – A Memorandum Providing Guidance to Local Authorities on Recycling, HMSO, 1991.

APPENDIX 3   'THE TRUE COST OF LANDFILL – ENERGY RECYCLING IS STRONG COMPETITOR'

[Reprinted from 'The true cost of landfill – energy recycling is strong competitor', *Warmer Bulletin*, Summer 1989]

A fair comparison of overall costs of waste disposal options needs to consider future expenditure and income in present-day values. Britain's *Waste Managment Paper No 26* applied discounted cash flow (DCF) to a landfill taking 1 000 000 tonnes per day of MSW at mid-1984 prices. Rod Taylor of the DoE re-examines the figures contained in *WMP26* and finds that UK landfill is likely to cost at least £16 per tonne today, putting energy-from-waste schemes into strong competition.

Waste management in the UK is approaching an annual turnover of £5000m. Some £1000m of that is in the municipal sector, with refuse collection accounting for about two-thirds of the total. Local authority collection, treatment and disposal should really be optimised as an entity, argues Mr. Taylor. 'It's no earthly use getting the cheapest disposal system if you are simply piling on the cost of collection.'

Arriving at an accurate cost per tonne of refuse handled is often difficult because so much MSW is not weighed. 'Who, other than a waste management practitioner, would dream of dealing on a 'cost per tonne' basis with a commodity which is not properly weighed?' asks Mr. Taylor.

Waste Management Paper (WMP) 26 used DCF for a clay-basin landfill of 13.6 ha, 15 metres deep, taking 100 000 tonnes per annum for 20 years, and arrived at £3.52 per tonne. No allowance was made for land acquisition and only a small charge allocated to passive gas venting.

In his proposal, Mr. Taylor adds 25% to 1984 prices and recalculates on the basis of an initial outlay of £1 per cubic metre for an air-space of two million cubic metres, and a 'trivial' credit of £2400 per ha for reclaimed land when it no longer requires aftercare – in year 37! Gas venting adds £300 000.

Using the current discount rate of 8% recommended by the UK Treasury for cash flow and waste input, rather than the 5% of WMP 26, he arrives at a December 1988 landfill cost of £7.25 per tonne. Mr. Taylor then assumes an in-place refuse density of 0.8 tonnes per cubic metre as a more credible average than the 1 tonne per cubic metre of the Paper, and increases site dimensions to accommodate the same quantity of waste. With adjustments to related factors, this pushes DCF cost to £9.05 per tonne.

On top of this must come the cost of transporting refuse to the tip face, an expense often not fully understood. Driver's time at £15 per hour (including overheads) for a reasonable round trip of 20 miles per hour, and £0.75 per payload-tonne per mile for the vehicle, adds £5 per tonne of waste handled, as follows:

$$\frac{£15 + (0.75p \times 20 \text{ miles})}{6 \text{ tonnes payload}}$$

Adding £2 per tonne for wear and tear on collection vehicle site use in lieu of site transport, brings the total to £16 per tonne.

Future provision against LFG and escape of chlorinated or organic solvents into aquifers might call for more than conventional clay barriers. Mr. Taylor postulates a double skin of steel sheet piling enclosing impermeable clay or bentonite for extra protection. Driven five metres into the ground with one metre protruding as a visible safeguard, this would cost £2400 per metre run. Since the projected site is now of 18.2 ha, the barrier would add £4m to engineering costs. A further £100 000 would be required if gas venting and monitoring of the inner filling were to be specified.

Simple arithmetic would divide this £4.1m by 100 000 tonnes of refuse for 20 years and result in just over £2 per tonne extra. DCF provides a more realistic £4.4 per tonne and pushes the overall total to £20–£21 per tonne.

The same 100 000 tonne per annum through an WDF plant, assuming all pellets are sold at £10 per tonne ex-works, represents about £24 for every tonne handled. Inciner-ation with power generation would reach about £38 per tonne. Other current disposal operations, based on quoted figures and estimates, show costs per tonne as follows:

London river transport	£25
London road transport	£15
London rail transport	£20
Aveley landfill gate fee	£4.50–£5 (with gas income)
Edmonton incinerator	£10.50
East Sussex road transport	£15
Rural district	£5–£7 (no gas income)

Tighter control of landfill and higher engineering costs will create opportunities for the sophisticated treatments at present limited to population centres generating at least 200 000 tonnes of waste per year.

ANSWERS TO SELF-ASSESSMENT QUESTIONS

SAQ 1

The NRA has a duty under the 1989 Water Act to protect the quality of ground water and conserve its use for water resources. Ground water provides 35% of present public demand and in many areas is the only available future resource. It also provide supplies for many private abstractors. Ground water also feeds surface waters through springs and base flow to rivers. Surface and ground water are bound together in the water cycle (see Units 5–6).

If ground water becomes polluted, it is very difficult to rehabilitate. It may take decades before an aquifer can be restored to use. Prevention is better than having a polluted aquifer, hence the emphasis on scrutiny of all waste disposal applications by the NRA before a licence is issued and after site closure to ensure that adequate water protection measures have been implemented. Where necessary, a groundwater monitoring regime may be required.

SAQ 2

The 'duty of care' under the EPA is applicable to all who have any dealings with controlled waste. They must take all reasonable measures to prevent unlicensed waste deposits, or breaches of a licence. The treatment, keeping or disposal of controlled wastes must be carried out as in the licence. No pollution of the environment or harm to human health is permitted. Waste must not escape at any link in the chain and must only be transferred to an authorised person or to 'a person for authorised transport.'

A written description of the waste is required which sets out its chemical analysis and properties and the safety precautions to be observed.

SAQ 3

Potential forms of pollution:

From landfill operation – noise, odours, polluted water, landfill gas, litter, vermin, gulls (and their droppings), vehicle movements, loss of good agricultural land, greenhouse effect enhancement, loss of sites of scientific or ecological interest.

From incineration – noise, vehicle movements, chimney intrusion on skyline, air pollution, ash disposal problem.

From recycling operations – noise, odours, vermin, litter, vehicle movements, unsightly heaps of materials.

All waste-related operations have potential environmental impacts. Their impacts can be controlled and minimised but this costs money and needs careful planning, implementation and monitoring during and afterwards to recognised standards by qualified personnel. Independent auditing is to be recommended.

SAQ 4

Assuming *all* the waste paper in Table 2 is collected, the respective amounts per 1000 households are:

Houses and bungalows	3.6 tonnes per week
Multi-storey flats	1.86 tonnes per week
Tenements	2.15 tonnes per week

If the wastepaper had a market which achieved a net income (i.e. after collection costs have been covered), then bungalow land is the place to go. My household is at the high end of the above as I 'produce' over 5 kg of waste paper per week. Not all waste paper is recyclable.

SAQ 5

The respective percentages of each waste component are taken from Table 1 and multiplied by the appropriate calorific value. The contributions are:

Dust and cinders	$0.068 \times 9.6 = 0.6528$
Vegetable	$0.28 \times 6.7 = 1.876$
Paper	$0.306 \times 14.6 = 4.4676$
Rag	$0.019 \times 16 = 0.304$
Plastics	$0.084 \times 37 = 3.108$
Unclassified	$0.072 \times 17.6 = 1.2672$
Total	11.6756 MJ

(a) 11.7 MJ kg^{-1} (rounded off). (Note that the moisture content of the vegetable matter, and its percentage, is highly variable: 10.5 MJ kg^{-1} is a normal figure. Note also the contribution that the plastics content makes. One school of thought is that the energy content of the oil used to make the plastics should be recovered by using plastics as a fuel for heat and power production.

(b) The percentage of the CV of industrial coal is

$$\frac{11.7}{28} \times 100 = \text{approx. } 42\%$$

These are gross calorific values (use set book for explanation).

SAQ 6

From Table 1, there is in theory 30.6% waste paper available, which means that if all waste paper were eliminated from the waste, 153 000 tonnes per year ($0.306 \times 500\,000$) would be eliminated. This would theoretically produce a disposal cost saving of £2 295 000 per year.

However, this assumes that all paper can be sold (definitely not the case) or that a marketable fuel can be made. Also, the costs of collecting the waste paper or making the fuel would have to be less than the disposal cost savings for this scheme to be economically viable. Waste paper costs money to collect and if there is no market for the paper (as is often the case) then the proposal could end up costing the council tax payers millions of pounds. For example, if the net cost of collecting the waste paper were £25 per tonne (and this is quite possible) then the scheme would cost (£25 × 153 000) or £3 825 000 per year. Recycling can be a costly business particularly if, as is widely anticipated, the market for waste paper continues to be oversupplied from either continental Europe or the USA (as well as having surplus UK waste paper). This points up the need for a spectrum of waste management solutions (see Section 1.1). In practice, not all paper is reclaimable owing to contamination, lack of markets and costs (as this exercise makes plain).

SAQ 7

The percentage of returnable bottles (1980–90) has declined from 15.8% to 1.5%, a 90.5% reduction using 1980 as a base. Refer to Figure 28. From this extrapolation, roughly 0.5% of the take-home beer market might be in returnable bottles by 1995. Note: extrapolation to small quantities is difficult, but look at the trend – a 77% reduction in 10 years.

SAQ 8

SAQ 7 shows that the ten-year decline in the case of returnable beer bottles is

$$\frac{15.8 - 1.5}{15.8} \times 100 = 90.5\%$$

For soft drinks over the same ten-year period, the percentage reduction is

$$\frac{48 - 11}{48} \times 100 = 77\%$$

so the *rate* of decline in returnable bottle use for take-home beer and soft drinks is different.

SAQ 9

The principal changes in domestic waste over the last 100 years can be briefly summarised as: ash reduced from almost 80% (1879) to about 5% (1989); vegetable and putrescible content increased from 10% (1979) to about 30% (1989); metals, glass (and non-plastics) rose from negligible (1879) to 7.6, 9.5 and 8.9% respectively (1989); and paper rose from roughly 6% to 30% in the same interval.

The changes were prompted by central heating, increase in packaging, development and use of plastics. Less composting and scavenging of waste compared with 1879. Greater profligacy, hence more food wasted.

What can we expect 100 years hence? I wonder!

The main effect on landfill (see Table 1) is that waste compaction is much more difficult to achieve. This necessitates the use of special compactors to squeeze the plastic bottles, cans, packaging, etc., down to acceptable site densities so that the landfill space is used efficiently and settlement is minimised on completion of tipping. Site stabilisation may take up to 50 years (with the evolution of landfill gas from the decay of organic materials also continuing apace).

SAQ 10

Using Darcy's law:

$$Q = kAi$$

$$= 10^{-6} \times 5000 \times \frac{1}{20} \text{ m}^3 \text{ d}^{-1}$$

$$= 2.5 \times 10^{-4} \text{ m}^3 \text{ d}^{-1}$$

$$= 9.1 \times 10^{-2} \text{ m}^3 \text{ year}^{-1}$$

This is miniscule, and it explains the attraction of old clay-lined pits as landfill sites (if the clay is thick and homogeneous).

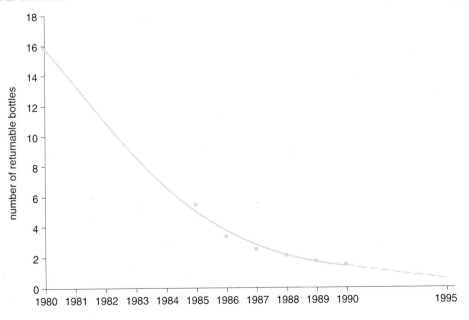

Figure 28 *For SAQ 7.*

SAQ 11

(a) The rate of reduction in flow rate with clay thickness decreases markedly. However, at less than 4–5 m thickness the flow rate drops quickly as the thickness increases.

(b) An increase of permeability by a factor of 10, i.e. from 10^{-6} to 10^{-5} m d^{-1}, has a marked effect on leachate flow rate. (New EC measures are expected to specify very low permeabilities for landfill sites.)

SAQ 12

Figure 29 shows cross-sections of the three types of site. In a containment site (Figure 29a), the leachate is contained within the site by the impermeable clays. In a slow attenuation site (Figure 29b), the sand and gravel allows slow leachate migration with significant attenuation. The underlying homogeneous stratum protects deeper aquifers. In an insignificant attenuation site (Figure 29c), the fissured strata allow rapid leachate migration into the aquifer, with possibly insignificant attenuation.

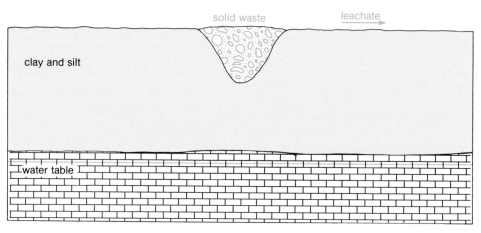

(a) containment

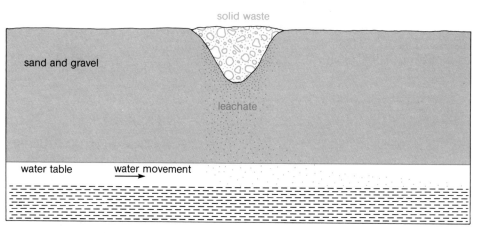

(b) slow attenuation

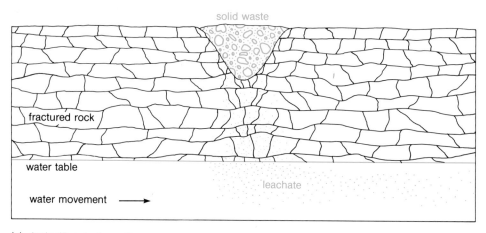

(c) insignificant attenuation

Figure 29 *Main classes of landfill site.*

SAQ 13

$$\text{organic matter} + \text{oxygen} \xrightarrow{\text{microorganisms}} CO_2 + H_2 + NH_3 + \text{energy}$$

SAQ 14

(a) From the text, the calorific value of LFG (45% methane) is $16\,000$ kJ m^{-3} (normal). Hence 1 tonne MSW produces LFG whose total fuel value is $350 \times 16\,000$ kJ = 5600 MJ, if all of it can be collected.

(b) The calculated CV of 1 tonne MSW (from SAQ 5) is 1000×11.7 MJ = 11 700 MJ. Thus we can see that LFG route to energy is not as good as burning MSW for a fuel; all other things being equal, there is an energy deficit of $(11\,700 - 5600) = 6100$ MJ t^{-1} MSW. This is due to some portions of the MSW (e.g. coated paper, plastics) not being converted to LFG.

(c) If 30% of the LFG can be extracted for fuel (this is a typical value) then only (0.30×5600) MJ t^{-1} is available, i.e. 1680 MJ. This is only (1680/11 700) or 14% of the fuel energy available from using MSW as a fuel in a specially constructed incinerator or energy recycling plant. In practice, LFG can be burnt more efficiently than MSW in an incinerator, hence the factor may rise to >14%.

(d) Burning MSW in an energy-from-waste plant is a much more efficient method of utilising all the energy content of MSW, rather than 'converting' it to LFG in a landfill site and then burning the gas for energy recovery afterwards.

SAQ 15

The adoption of high-density baling will extend the landfill site life by

$$\frac{1000 - 650}{650} \times 100 = 54\%$$

As the landfill (non-baling) has a total capacity for

$$200\,000 \times \frac{650}{1000} = 130\,000 \text{ tonnes}$$

or 13 years at $10\,000$ t yr^{-1}, then baling will give an extra 7 years of life on the basis of this calculation.

SAQ 16

(a) Permeability 10^{-9} m sec^{-1}; 2-m thickness. The lower the permeability the less the likelihood of leachate leakage; 2-m thickness is an optimum, as the effects of greater thickness are marginal at a permeability of 10^{-9} m s^{-1}.

(b) On 1 m thickness at permeability of 10^{-9} m s^{-1}, the discharge value is roughly 0.2 l d^{-1}, whereas on 1-m thickness at a permeability of 10^{-7} m s^{-1}, the discharge value is roughly 17 l d^{-1}. This is an increase of 8400%.

SAQ 17

Incineration	Landfill
air pollution	landfill gas
noise	water pollution
vehicle movements	vehicle movements
visual intrusion	vermin

This is my list. However, if we extended it, more elements common to both would appear (e.g. noise, visual intrusion) as well as vehicle movements.

SAQ 18

The incinerator could be overloaded, the bed-depth too great for the time spent in the combustion chamber, the air supply insufficient (unlikely), or the sample could be unrepresentative, or the test procedures could be defective or misunderstood by those conducting the tests (or it is a clapped-out pre-1896 ancient British incinerator that should have been shut down years ago!).

SAQ 19

From the set book (Table 9), the EC requirement for dust is 30 mg m^{-3} (normal) and for HCl 50, HF 2.0, SO$_2$ 300 mg m^{-3} (normal) respectively. Munich North is at least 5 mg m^{-3} (normal) better on particulates, meets the HCl requirements, is 200 mg m^{-3} (normal) better on SO$_2$ and is <1 mg m^{-3} (normal) for HF, so it meets or exceeds the EC requirements using the semi-dry method.

The HMIP requirements as at 1992 for all new UK incineration plant and existing plant after 1996 are reproduced in Table 24. (Semi-dry scrubbing and particulate removal by 'bag' filters can meet these stringent requirements.)

Table 24   *Concentration limits for releases from contained sources*

Total particulate matter	30 mg m^{-3}
Volatile organic compounds (excluding particulate matter)	20 mg m^{-3}
Sulphur dioxide	300 mg m^{-3}
Oxides of nitrogen (expressed as nitrogen dioxide)	350 mg m^{-3}
Hydrogen chloride	30 mg m^{-3}
Hydrogen fluoride	2 mg m^{-3}
Carbon monoxide (hourly)	100 mg m^{-3}
Carbon monoxide (95% of all measurements in any 24 hours)	150 mg m^{-3}
Dioxins (TEQ)	1 ng m^{-3}
Arsenic, chromium, copper, lead, manganese, nickel and tin	1.0 mg m^{-3}
Cadmium	0.1 mg m^{-3}
Mercury	0.1 mg m^{-3}

Reference conditions for concentrations of substances in emissions to air are: temperature 273 K (0 °C), pressure 101.3 kPa (1 atmosphere), 11% vol. per vol. oxygen, dry gas. A temperature of at least 850 °C for at least two seconds in the presence of at least 6% oxygen, after the last injection of combustion air, is required.

Source: HMIP (1992) Process Guidance Note IPR 5/3.

SAQ 20

(a) From set book Figure 52, the fly ash weighs 40 kg in a total residue discharge of 270 kg, i.e. approximately 15%, or 0.4% of total input (some plants achieve 0.29%).

(b) The total weight of ash is 270 kg which contains $40 \times (0.2/100)$ kg cadmium, i.e. 0.08 kg Cd. Hence the percentage of Cd in the mixed ash is $(0.08/270) \times 100$ = 0.03%.

SAQ 21

(a) 2.38 tonnes of MSW are consumed per MWh produced for sale.

(b) As the waste has a CV of 10 500 MJ t^{-1}, then the fuel energy to generate 1 MWh is

$10\,500 \times 2.38$ MJ = 24 990 MJ.

$$\text{overall thermal efficiency} = \frac{1\ \text{MWh}}{24\,990\ \text{MJ}} \times 100$$

$$= \frac{1\,000\,000 \times 60 \times 60 \times 100}{24\,990 \times 1\,000\,000}\ \%$$

$$= 14.4\%$$

(c) The efficiency could be increased to roughly 70% if district heating were used as well. This option is to be employed in the new 400 000 t yr^{-1} MSW incinerator for south-east London which will provide both power and heat for roughly 50 000 dwellings in south-east London.

(d) Gross income (for 6.5p per kWh)

$= £144\,744 \times 1000 \times (6.5/100)$

$= £9.41$ million per year.

SAQ 22

The environmental effects schedule shows that any air pollutants emitted will meet EC requirements. Landfill (as at 1992) does not have to meet any requirements for emission levels of LFG. Visual intrusion is negligible because of use of existing buildings. New buildings would be a different matter. New landfill sites require careful screening. However, if land draining is attempted, then there could be a substantial intrusion. MSW combustion produces CO$_2$. Landfill produces LFG whose methane content is a powerful greenhouse agent, only 30% of which can be collected. Noise from the project is to be kept to DoE limits (see discussion in Units 11–13).

SAQ 23

(a) From Table 20, GCV coal is 27 GJ t^{-1} and GCV WDF is 18 GJ t^{-1}. Hence

price per GJ for coal is $\dfrac{50}{27} = £1.852$

price per GJ for WDF is $\dfrac{20}{18} = £1.11$

(b) Coal efficiency = 78%, hence

price per GJ from boiler is $\dfrac{1.852}{0.78} = £2.374$

WDF efficiency = 76%, hence

price per GJ from boiler $= \dfrac{1.111}{0.76} = £1.462$

(c) Boiler size = 5 MW. Over 1 year the boiler delivers

$$\frac{30}{100} \times 5 \times 60 \times 60 \times 24 \times 365 \text{ MJ} = 47\ 304 \text{ GJ}$$

This requires $\frac{47\ 304}{0.78 \times 27}$ = 2246.1 tonnes coal

or $\frac{47\ 304}{0.76 \times 18}$ = 3457.9 tonnes WDF

Annual ash production from WDF = $\frac{14}{100} \times 3457.9$
$$= 484.1 \text{ tonnes}$$

Annual ash production from coal = $\frac{5}{100} \times 2246.1$
$$= 112.3 \text{ tonnes}$$

Hence, extra ash requiring disposal = 371.8 tonnes.

SAQ 24

(a)   Input = 18 t h^{-1}

Fines = 6.3 t h^{-1}

Fe metals = 0.9 t h^{-1}

WDF = 5.2 t h^{-1}

Total sold =12.4 t h^{-1}

In addition, 1 t h^{-1} H$_2$O is evaporated, and 0.4 t h^{-1} WDF is combusted in the drier, i.e. a total of 13.8 t h^{-1}. This leaves $(18 - 13.8) = 4.2$ t h^{-1} for disposal or 23% of input.

(b) (i)   Fines are 9% (of input) greater than the assumed analysis (35% − 26%)

(ii)   Ferrous metals (output) are 2% less than the assumed analysis. Also the paper and board and plastics totals 43%. This could be assumed to be totally available for WDF production which is only 29%, i.e. an apparent 14% shortfall.

(iii)   Examination of the flow sheet shows that 6.6 t h^{-1} or 36% of the input waste enters the drier where 1 t h^{-1} of water is evaporated, leaving 5.6 t h^{-1} or 32% of input waste, of which a further 0.4 t h^{-1}

(2%) is used to fuel the drier, giving a net output of 5.2 t h^{-1} or 29% of input. Not all the combustible materials are recovered but this is a reasonable performance. Some of the other 'losses' take place in the heavy fraction stream which will remove some of the metals and large unprocessed paper or plastic objects.

SAQ 25

Compost at 100 tonnes per day requires a bulk volume of 200 m^3 per day. If the compost is stored in 2 m layers, an area of $(6 \times 7 \times 100)$ m^2 = 4200 m^2 is required for 6 weeks storage. If a factor of 2 is used for space to allow materials handling (i.e. turning and aeration of the compost), the area required is 8400 m^2, 0.84 ha (about 2 acres). This area must be concreted, and the leachate collected and treated. (It may even need to be enclosed.)

SAQ 26

(100% − (fuel 39% + compost 34.8%)) = 26.2%. If all the glass and metals could be recycled, this would leave 8.2% for landfill. An idealised scenario!

SAQ 27

The completed revenue table is shown in Table 25. You might like to put in your own household waste survey figures in column (a) and use the values in columns (b) and (d) to see what answer you get.

Note that glass and aluminium total £2.82 out of the £5.18 overall figure. Both of these constituents (and the ferrous metals) can be recovered without lowering the calorific value (and perhaps improving it) of the MSW as a fuel.

Examination of the table shows that glass and aluminium total 2.74 or 55% of the recovered materials income. (Both are eminently suitable for recovery through glass and can banks respectively.)

Table 25

	Weight/ (kg per house per year)	Estimated clean fraction/ %	Clean weight/ (kg per house per year)	Possible merchant price (£ per tonne)	Revenue potential per household per year (£)
	a	b	c: (a × b)/100	d	e
Paper	200	60	120	5	0.60
Plastic film	24	60	14.4	30	0.43
Dense plastic	18	70	12.6	60	0.76
Textiles	24	50	12	10	0.12
Glass	60	90	54	30	1.62
Ferrous metal	42	80	33.6	10	0.34
Aluminium	4	70	2.8	400	1.12
Total					4.99

SAQ 28

Recycling may be encouraged by:

- subsidies to reclaimers;

- a disposal tax which makes (say) landfill much more expensive, hence recycling waste reduces the amount of tax paid;

- virgin materials tax: excess virgin materials (or energy) consumption attracts a surcharge;

- product specification for reuse;

- deposit legislation for drinks containers (Sweden has achieved well over 80% return of aluminium cans through deposit legislation);

- design for dismantling and reuse, e.g. car parts;

- educating the public, especially schoolchildren;

- banning of non-returnable beverage containers.

SAQ 29

(a) $0.4 + 1.6 + (10 \times 0.7) = 9 \text{ kWh}_e$ (where $\text{kWh}_e = 1$ kilo-watt-hour of electricity)

(b) $10 \times 1.9 = 19 \text{ kWh}_e$

(c) 10 kWh_e

(d) 30% less manufacturing energy means $0.7 \times 1.1 = 0.77$ kWh_e is used in manufacture,

hence total energy $= 0.6 + 0.77 + 0.2 = 1.57 \text{ kWh}_e$

Ten bottles $= 10 \times 1.57 = 15.7 \text{ kWh}_e$

(e) $15.7 - 9 = 6.7 \text{ kWh}_e$

SAQ 30

Difficulties with contamination (e.g. oils, paints, foodstuffs).

Difficulties with mixtures, e.g. PVC, PET, polystyrene, LDPE, HDPE.

Separation costs are high for the value of the collected materials. (Refer to cost calculations and data in Table 22.)

Usually mixed plastic products can only be manufactured into low quality objects such as plastic fence posts. These do not command the high prices of products made from uncontaminated plastics.

Figure 69 of the set book shows how one French method of tackling PVC bottle recycling is through selective collection and sorting to produce secondary products, i.e. non food use plastic products such as pipes and fencing. Note that, of the 75% throughput, only 50 tonnes comes directly from domestic waste. This keeps impurity levels down.

SAQ 31

One tonne polyethylene requires 18.7 tonnes of crude oil, whereas 1 tonne PVC requires 8 tonnes. Hence, in energy terms, PVC is a much less energy intensive material and therefore has an inbuilt cost advantage.

The presence of plastics in MSW raises the CV of the waste substantially and as it is very difficult to separate out the various plant components of MSW at a reasonable cost, incineration with energy recovery or 'energy recycling' is one way of releasing the energy content of the plastic waste for useful purposes. The incineration process produces a dense ash which is easily landfilled as opposed to low density MSW which needs special compaction machinery to collect landfill. A 90% volume reduction is achieved by incineration.

SAQ 32

(a) £55 t^{-1}.

(b) Change in cost factor $= (30/15) = 2$, hence net cost per tonne of recyclables becomes £40 t^{-1}.

(c) £30 t^{-1}. (This, as we have seen, is 'high'.)

SAQ 33

(a) From Figure 24, the 64-oz glass bottle produces 5306.1 lbs of waste per 1000 gallons. The 8.45-oz drink box produces 731.9 lbs waste. Therefore, if there is no glass recycling,

$$\% \text{ waste reduction} = \frac{5306.1 - 731.9}{5306.1}$$

$$= 86.21\%$$

(b) If there is 50% glass recycling, then using the drink box gives

$$\% \text{ waste reduction} = \frac{2653.05 - 731.9}{2653.05}$$

$$= 72.41\%$$

(iii) 50% glass recycling produces 2653 lbs of waste. The 64-oz plastic bottle produces 2123.3 lbs waste. Hence the glass and plastic figures are comparable. Note these are Coca-Cola's figures. But we can still do the arithmetic on them! This shows that the recycling rate is a very important factor in comparing packaging systems and why it is vital for the glass industry to increase its recycling percentage and/or for us to use returnable refillable bottles.

SAQ 34

See Table 26.

Table 26

Class	Household products	Home improvement	Lawn and garden	Automotive
Corrosive	Laundry and stain removers	Paint stripper	Most swimming pool chemicals	Acid batteries
	Toilet cleaners		Slug killer	
	Floor wax stripper		Fertilisers	
	Drain cleaners			
	Oven cleaners			
	Some bathroom cleaners			
	Bleach			
Flammable	Furniture cleaner	Acetone	Insect repellent	All aerosol cans
	All aerosol cans	Contact cement	Camping fuel	Waste oil
	Hobby chemicals	Paint brush cleaner and solvents	Petrol	
		All aerosol cans	All aerosol cans	
Toxic	Isopropyl alcohol	Wood stain	Dandelion, weed, insect and grass killers	Radiator coolant and antifreeze
	Hobby chemicals	Wood preservative	Fertilisers	Waste oil
	Batteries (nicad, alkaline, carbon)	Varnish remover	Malathion (insecticide)	
		Turpentine	Camping fuel	
		Paint thinner		
Reactive	All aerosol cans	All aerosol cans	All aerosol cans	All aerosol cans
	Bleach with any acid or base	Fertilisers	Barbecue and camping fuels	
			Propane cylinders	

SAQ 35

1 *Reduce*

Try alternatives that produce less waste or harmful residues, e.g. water based paint instead of oil based.

Don't purchase more products than you really need.

Use up dangerous products before throwing them out.

Give leftovers to those who can use them.

Use pressure-treated timber for outdoor purposes. It lasts five times longer.

2 *Reuse*

Many chemical products have alternative uses: use old paint as primer.

Allow used turpentine to sit in a sealed jar until paint particles settle. Pour off clear liquid and use again.

Don't buy several products if one can do the job. General household cleaners can clean a variety of dirt. Check product labels.

3 *Recycle*

Used motor oil can be treated and used again.

Car batteries can be recycled.

Return spent mercury/cadmium batteries to point of purchase for disposal.

Return old refrigerators or deep freezers to a local authority CFC removal depot, usually at civic amenity sites.

Give old clothing to charity shops.

4 *Dispose*

Separate hazardous materials from your household waste and dispose of them via approved methods, e.g. batteries to collection points.

Don't dispose of hazardous materials in sewer systems, storm drains, soil or open bodies of water.

Don't put surgical 'sharps' or medical waste in ordinary household waste: inform your collection authority.